To Momma and Daddy

CAROLINA COMFORT

Third Edition

by

Karen E. Dodd

Karen E. Dodd

Published by:
Karen Dodd
dkdodd1@suddenlink.net

© 2007 Karen Dodd

ISBN: 0-9707197-4-4
Carolina Comfort
Third Edition

Books by Karen Dodd

Carolina Comfort
Carolina Comfort II
Down East on Nelson Island

Acknowledgement

The birth of my grandchildren and the death of my parents urged me to record memories about growing up in North Carolina. This is my way to express love and appreciation to my parents, Samuel Burgin and Sarah Rhyne Kale, grandmothers, aunts, great aunts and the rest of my family. It is a way to share them with this family's children, tomorrow.

The recent death of my sister due to muscular dystrophy is another reason to record our stories. Perhaps some day this horrible gene will be nullified by medicine or family metamorphosis. In the meantime, we need to leave a warning about this trait that travels from mother to daughter through our blood line.

The contrast between being the daughter of a Coast Guardsman and daughter of the South visiting my grandmother, Coral Rhyne, in her century-old home in piedmont North Carolina never confused me. I merely played different roles depending on whether I was in Morehead City or Mt. Holly.

Kate Burgin Kale was my father's mother. She also had a profound affect on my life. My Dear Miss Kate tells her story.

My husband, Denton, supports me by proof reading or doing the dishes when I want to write. I am forever grateful for his patience. I also thank my friends: Dot Fleming and Rachel Smith for their encouragement.

My Southern heritage nourishes and blesses me.

Write you family stories.

Karen Elizabeth Kale Dodd, middle sister of three, daughter of a youngest sister of three!

Sarah Rhyne, Karen Elizabeth, Patricia Anne

Introduction

When I gave a copy of this book to my mother for Christmas the year before she died, she read it and said, "Lord-a-mercy, where did you get these stories? I don't remember them, Karen!"

So perhaps the years played tricks on my mind. I blame it on time and dreams that may have twisted the growing up spell of youth.

I wrote the book to remind you of the South from the 1940's to the 1960's. I share my memories, smells, sounds, and feelings. Perhaps this will churn up pictures for you.

The mid portion of Carolina Comfort I comes from my experiences in the late twentieth century.

To complement the memories of the mid and late twentieth century, I include My Dear Miss Kate: a Postcard Story, a glimpse of the early 1900's in western North Carolina. These postcards, tucked in a brown paper sack, were among my grandmother's treasures when she died. I placed them in a photo album with two-sided plastic pockets. If you look through the book, you can admire their rich colors and distinctive handwriting.

With the use of a computer, I put them in chronological order. The narrative

comes from research and stories from my
Daddy and Granny Kale.

Table of Contents

Granny's Front Porch

My Granny's front porch is wide enough to
hold a dozen dark green slatted rocking
chairs. Smooth round columns stand on
brick shoulders lifting the roof aloft, like a
preacher holds up a baptized child for the
congregation to see. The roof is high enough
to catch the late summer breeze that shifts
above the boxwoods and hydrangeas, cool
enough to keep the heat away from the 100-
year old brick home.

It's a quiet place to swing away the
evening, watch lightning bugs while listening
to crickets, or doves cooing beneath the
eaves. The horse chestnuts and dogwoods
turn to lace in the spring. At Christmas, the
tall cedar and holly trees guard against
winter doldrums.

My Granny's porch is long enough to be a raceway for grandchildren on their painted rocking horses or the pedal-pushed racing coupe.

"No running on the porch!"

Many times the porch served up tables of home-cooked family reunion meals: fried chicken, country ham biscuits, watermelon and cantaloupe, chow-chow, bread and butter pickles, warm yeast rolls hot from that double oven range in the kitchen. Deviled eggs, potato salad, baked beans, tomatoes still warm from the garden, sliced into the Blue Willow dish. Coconut cake made from scratch, shredded coconut spilling onto the table, damson pies, beside peach cobbler, and cookies for the younger ones.

"Don't make a mess."

A two-person swing sways at the far end where my parents courted. Cool stone steps lead down to the portico. It's a great place to watch Easter-egg hunts or football games played with enthusiasm in the front yard, and listen to memories retold.

It's also a working porch. String beans, shuck corn, slice the kernels – making a sloppy mess of creamed corn or the beginnings for applesauce. There's a good light for quilting piece goods, tearing out a seam, or hemming a skirt while

grandchildren sprawl out with comic books:
Wonder Woman, Superman, Little Lulu,
Archie and the Lone Ranger.

"Wanna swap?"

Granny swept the porch each
morning. She pulled her hair up with combs
and pins, fashioned in a bun at the back of
her neck. She wore a big-pocketed apron
when she emptied her pans of dishwater
around the azaleas because the sun steamed
away the dampness from the earth. Granny
made geraniums bloom over night, pinching
off the dull blooms, clipping off browned
tips of ferns, and shooing the old cat that
was avoiding her kittens.

"Scat cat!"

The hired man came to knock down
hornet nests under the eaves. Granny fed
him a simple meal on the porch.

"Otto, you want some buttermilk?"

We grew up and fled to our own
homes – far away. My uncle lives in the
house now. We have reunions when the
family gathers under the eaves of that porch.
Most of my aunts, uncles and Daddy passed.
My granddaughter walked the same porch I
walked as a child, with her great-
grandmother watching. She played in the sun
where I once climbed onto a merry-go-
round and rode with my cousins. I imagine
Granny swaying in that porch swing watching

whose left of her children, grandchildren and their grandchildren. Her gartered stockings, rolled to her knees, peek out from her flowered dress. She nudges the floor to get the swing a-swaying. She smiles, "Do you remember the time...?"

Granny would sit and rock with me in the swing. She read me The Little Red Hen and Peter Pan. I looked at the pictures and listened to her voice lull me towards drowsiness.

Granny no longer comes to the porch in her flowered shirtwaist dress and sensible leather shoes.

I wish I could send my granddaughter to lie on the chaise lounge of that porch, to read Nancy Drew, The Black Stallion, Treasure Island, and Little Women among the soft cushions. My mother would call me inside.

"I want to finish this chapter first."

Now I'm looking for a place to retire. It will have a swing or a glider, a place to eat meals, enjoy company, and a place to doze in the sun. I want a cool evening breeze to drive away the mosquitoes and a sunny place to sit on winter days. A place my grandchildren will come to read. I want a slow moving ceiling fan and flowers, a chaise lounge and chairs - maybe green slatted ones.

Affirmative Action

There were no black children where I went to school. There were no brown, tan, yellow, or red children either. The children who came to my school had both mommies and daddies. They lived in homes with a black and white television and one car. No one smelled of kerosene. No one had head lice. No one came to school without breakfast. No abused child showed bruises or broken bones. Or at least I never knew of any.

Where I went to school, no Blacks attended our class. There were no women principals, governors, or senators. No Hispanic council members reigned. There were no Asian business people. No Catholic was President of the United States in the 1950's. Women, minorities, Muslims, and

Jews weren't visible in power or business positions where I lived.

We learned cursive writing on teacher-drawn lines on the chalkboard. We collected coins for Liberty Stamps and purchased U. S. Savings Bonds. We loved our country. No one burned our flag. We pledged our allegiance to "one nation" without the "under God" words. We read the Bible each morning. We memorized verses for recitation.

There were no Blacks where I went to school. There was no handicapped "mainstreaming" either. There were no dropouts. They "moved away." Mal-formed children stayed home behind closed doors.

We played ball on grassless fields behind brick buildings. If we could not run with a ball, catch a ball, or throw a ball, we stood last in line as team captains called out other children's names. We attended school in brick buildings with wooden floors, kept clean by a black janitor. There were no air conditioners. We sweated through hot spring and fall days. Radiators steamed up the plaster walls that flaked and crumbled in the summer. Large wooden blinds or sectional shades kept out the glare.

The library was crammed with musty, worn books, filmstrip canisters, and stubborn projectors. Classrooms smelled of pencil shavings, chalk, oiled wooden floors, and purple test papers. School lunch was soup and a peanut butter or pimento cheese sandwich. Friday was Fish Day.

But there were no Blacks where I went to school. There were fire drills on windless days. We stood in straight lines waiting to return to class. Our brown, red, and blond heads bobbed as we fidgeted. The principal walked about with a stopwatch clocking our exits. Teachers shook their heads over the lost class time.

Divided by reading ability, we were named blue birds, red birds, or yellow birds. No one was labeled a dummy or badgered by bullies. We stood in corners if we misbehaved. Assembly was held every Friday.

I told my daughter when she was in the first grade, "There were no black children where I went to school." In the 1970's, she sat at a table with a black child and a yellow child. She was a daughter of a divorced working mother. In her school, migrant children came and went in the spring, like the tides. She had a woman principal. Someone shot our only Catholic president. "No," I said, "no black children attended class when I went to school."

Her pale face looked up at mine. She had blond hair and green eyes. She asked, "Weren't there a lot of empty chairs?"*

* I write this remembering school of the 1950's. In the 1970's Black replaced Negro and Colored, before African American became politically correct. In this and other stories, forgive the child's voice, thoughts, and political incorrectness.

Great Aunts' Spiced Tea

My Granny's name is Coral. Pearl is her full
sister. Annie, Sarah, and 'Tine are Granny's
half sisters. 'Tine is short for Christine. Five
sisters became schoolteachers, born to a
daddy with no son. He was a schoolteacher,
too.

My great granddaddy built their
house, carving the date above the porch, in
1879. The sisters retired by the time I knew
them. Over the years one or more came to
live in their daddy's big white wooden house,
located a short distance from my
grandmother.

Like a sleeping cat, the porch
stretches out along two sides of the house.
In summer, ferns and geraniums stand in
pots held in wicker stands along the edge,
but in winter, the plants migrate to the
breakfast room inside.

I dread going to their house. There
are no toys. We're not allowed to play. I have

to visit every time I go to my Granny's house, especially at Christmas.

"Get ready, we have to be there soon!"

I shrug off Mommaa's command and climb the stairs to change clothes. I can't wear my dungarees. It isn't proper. In 1954, I remember choosing a red Cramerton plaid dress with a black velveteen collar. Momma made it. My big sister has one just like it, but today she wears something else. I grump down the stairs and shoulder into the nylon car coat Momma bought on sale last year. It isn't as baggy as it was when I first got it.

"Go change your shoes. Wear the leather lace-up ones, not the cowboy boots you wore in the pasture."

I climb the stairs one more time before leaving.

I expect a bunch of cats to walk across my feet and brush up against my legs. Not a bad feeling except that I have to sit properly, say "Yes Ma'am" and be on my best behavior.

"No lying on the floor. Don't run along the porch, no playing tag in the yard among the boxwoods and flat slate stones. Mind your manners and behave," Momma reminds me.

Like I was going to throw my dress over my head and squall like a baby. How embarrassing! The old piano smiles with yellow ivory teeth.

"No, you may not play it." Again another reminder, "Needlepoint chairs are not to be leaned back in."

Velveteen buttons corset the couch by the window. Lifeless lace doilies faint across every chair top.

My sister sits up straight, legs crossed at the ankles. She combs her hair back with a ribbon like a June Allison photograph in a drugstore magazine. Her perfect complexion and slender body already show the signs of adolescence.

Little brother swaggers about the room as only a 2-year-old can, gaining attention with his big brown eyes and grin. I plump down on a stool by the door. The barrette in my hair begins to slide.

Aged portraits stare down from flower nosegay wallpaper, darkened with age. Converted chandeliers shine through electric light globes. Freshly cut limbs of spruce, tied up with red plastic bows hang on every door. Dusty, unlit candles stand in attention on the sideboard. There's a step down into the kitchen, added after the house was built.

"Would you like some spiced tea and a cookie?"

Every year the same stale fruitcake and bland sugar cookies prop up themselves on a crystal plate, on top of the teacart. I peer among the selections. Didn't I find a hair last year? Was it from a cat or a little old lady?

Momma listens politely, answering questions when prompted. They really don't want to hear from her. They want someone to talk to beside themselves. Daddy sits and smiles, leaning back in the only comfortable chair in the room.

The Aunts reminisce of school years past, this boy or that girl, now men and women with children of their own. "Where are they now – Belmont, Lincolnton, Stanley?"

Their slender wrinkled hands smooth the fabric in their laps. They sit erect, feet together at the front of their chairs. No slip hangs from the edge of their dress, no rolled garter peeks from under their hem. Every blue or gray hair is in place. A spot of rouge cloaks each hollow cheek in vain. Their memories are keen on long ago school days, yet they misplace keys and forget where they parked their car.

The Aunts serve spiced tea in china cups with delicate flowers, gold lacing the rims.

"Do be careful not to drop anything."

I balance cup and saucer on my lap and select a cookie. I always hope for a chocolate surprise or anything but a cold fruit glob center. Hot spiced tea, not too sweet, burns my tongue. Tired cloves silt the bottom of my cup, not very appealing to a 7-year-old.

"Please don't blow across the cup, dear. It's so unladylike. Sit up straight. How is school? What do you want to be when you grow up?"

To Momma, as if I can't hear, "She is getting a little chubby, isn't she? Better watch that. The beaus don't go for fat little girls. She has such a pretty face."

I eat the cookie and smile. I wonder if it's possible to empty my cup into the potted tree by the door without being caught.

"Finish the tea, child." Nope.

I sneak another cookie when I take the dishes back to the kitchen. The stolen cookie tastes better than the offered one. This one has a powdered sugar coating. I pop the whole cookie in my mouth to avoid telltale sugar and crumbs on the front of my dress with the black velveteen collar. Lips purse shut as I crunch the licorice flavored cookie into nothingness. Watch my step back into the parlor. Listen to relatives talk politely, of ills past and present. Keep silent unless spoken to.

"Give me a hug before you go."

What is that smell? Denture breath or body odor, dresses worn too many times before cleaning, old wool, or old cat?

I race to the car and reach for the handle, shocking myself. The electricity snaps in the cold winter air when I touch the door. I climb into the back seat without slamming the door on my hand or a sibling.

Parents hang back on the porch and listen, their heads nodding, like the car's back window dog. The cats rub against their legs. It's cold. The vinyl seat sticks to my bare legs. Finally, another hug, a polite kiss on the cheek, and my parents come to the car. Spiced tea with the aunts is over again – until next year.

Fifty years pass. When I travel by the house, attending family reunions, I glimpse the white board house among the spruce trees, where they lived. Boxwoods still guard the front walk. The highway encroached into the front yard. A fast food chicken restaurant belches grease into the air. I don't know who lives in the house now. My Aunts and Granny passed. Those delicate painted teacups and crystal plates were packed in someone's attic or sold in yard sales. Wal-Mart wreaths hang from the front door during the holidays.

I don't attend teas anymore, nor do I have to sit erect and sip quietly discussing family news. We cousins wallow in belly laughs remembering those days.

I miss my aunts' correct etiquette, their polite hospitality. Whenever I smell boxwood, I return to their slate sidewalk. I yearn for an afternoon of spiced tea when the weather gets cold. I might even be tempted to nibble at bland fruit glob sugar cookies. I hold the memories of my aunts and their Carolina comfort in my heart.

Last year, I bought my granddaughter a delicately painted china tea set, the cups edged with thin gold lace. Who knows? Some day we might have tea together. We'll talk about school -- and what she wants to be when she grows up.

Vegetable Soup

The furnace kicks on. Frost covers the ground outside. Frying eggs pop and pans clatter in the kitchen.

"Wake up! Get out of that bed. We got things to do and don't you dig back under the covers." Daddy retreats down the hall to admonish the next child. "Get out'a that bed. Shake a leg."

The girl reaches for her flannel lined jeans laying in the bottom drawer.

"Outside work today and you better dress warmly."

Undershirt covers trainer bra, cotton underpants replace the plaid pajamas. Thick socks, maybe two pair in her cowboy boots, keep her feet warm and cut off the moisture that collects between her toes. The girl gobbles up sloppy eggs, scrapple, and toast with jam while Momma selects a large Dutch oven pot and sets it on the eye of the stove. All frozen remnants of meals past clunk into it. A ham bone and a bit of steak follow a small serving of meatloaf left over from last night. She slices a turnip along with an onion. A piece of Italian sausage adds to the medley. Chicken stock frozen in a plastic carton, okra put away last summer, canned tomatoes melt into the broth. The soup begins to heat on the low flame.

Outside brother and sisters pick up limbs and trash. A winter storm blew the creek beyond its banks during the night. A string of debris outlines the lower yard near the water's edge. Heavy rakes barely budge the stubborn marsh reeds that clutch the edge of the winter grass. Old bottles, cardboard, coiled fishing line and cork tangle amid a pile of pier planks.

No Saturday morning cartoons, there is no mall. Television is black and white. Homework done the night before. Memorize the books of the Bible as she rakes, "Deuteronomy, Joshua, Judges, Ruth, 1st Samuel...." What has the dog dug up? Some yucky piece of flesh and fur or is it feathers? It's hard to tell.

The screen door slams; Momma comes out with a load of wash to peg to the clothesline. "Don't run underneath the clean clothes. Get that dog away from me. What has he got in his mouth?"

The smaller girl grabs up the bag of clothespins, slings the empty clothesbasket over her back, and carries it back to the utility room that joins the house. Standing by the back door, she hears the pot lid's steamy rattle. Warm smells of thickened pot liquor and roots. A clang as the lid is lifted and bay leaves go in, potatoes, followed by some old rice found in the back of the refrigerator.

Neat piles of creek trash dot the yard. City garbage trucks don't make weekly pickups along the road, where we live. We burn our trash or haul it to the dump. There is a big fifty-gallon barrel on the edge of the creek used to burn the weekly trash. Daddy lights a match to the house rubbish, old newspapers, potato, and carrot peels stick to the paper grocery bags that lined the kitchen trash can. Empty cans and jars mix with a pile of creek refuse waiting beside the barrel. It sizzles as the flame works its way through thin papers, licking, and crackling as it grows.

Soon the creek piles are gone and there's time for roller-skating before lunch.

"Where is my skate key?"

"Hang it around your neck," big

sister chastises her.

Cowboy boots, metal skates, rough wool muffler, damp with the moist winter breath. She tries in vain to keep up with her big sister. Brother vanishes up the street with dog. She can't match the speed of her big sister. Dip at the end of the drive. No curbs. She is afraid of the speed and the dip.

Big sister taunts from the other side. It's so cold the fingers sting beneath the glove. A wool muffler knitted by an aunt becomes unraveled from her neck and trips her as she tries to skate alone. Ears ring with skate rollers; the wind picks up. Sunny blue skies gray as the sun disappears behind cold streaming clouds. The leather strap across the boot loosens and down she goes.

Big sister is off with a friend. The dog returns, still smelling of his earlier find, he edges up to try to lick the small girl's face and rub his head under her arm.

"You stink!" She hollers to no one, "I'm going inside." Books offer the younger sister a good retreat for the rest of the day.

"Come and get it. Where's your sister? The table needs to be set." Momma pours the milk into tall glasses.

Can the small girl get away with putting Daddy's buttermilk in the place of her big sister's regular milk? Steaming hot soup is ladled into the wide bowls. Sliced corn bread waits in a pie pan, butter in the blue dish. Peaches in heavy syrup cuddle into little bowls. Is that home-made Angel Food cake in the kitchen? Everyone comes to the table.

The meal is blessed.

What a face she makes! Big sister's mouth lined with the buttermilk's thick mustache frowns across the table.

Daddy winks at the younger girl. Sister glares at her with mouth still bitter from that first gulp.

"Gotcha." Smug grin. Don't look up. "Dip the spoon away from you. Brush it along the back edge of the bowl." First bite is so hot she wants to spit it out. The roof of her mouth scorches in protest. Taste buds, paralyzed by the initial bite, return after a gulp of cold milk, to try the various flavors of refrigerator past.

"Whoever finds the bay leaf must kiss the cook," Momma grins.

Crusts of cornbread wipe up second helpings. Family too full to enjoy the cake just yet. Afternoon snack, maybe.

She finds her favorite chair after the dishes are washed and dozes in the window seat. Saturday afternoon wrestling follows country bluegrass twang on the television.

She continues to read.

"Did you learn all the books of the Bible yet? Boy that was good homemade vegetable soup," Daddy sinks into his chair.

Another Saturday ends and tomorrow church and Sunday School. She drags her boots across the floor to her room. Bits and pieces of family life like the ingredients of the soup making a unique child for the world she finds another day.

Summer Tea at Aunt Jo's

Invitations are sent, handwritten of course.
Out come the crystal plates and cut glass
punch bowl from the corner cupboard's
bowels. "The garden looks best in the
spring but early summer will do." Invitees
include DAR, book club, bridge club, the
aunts, sisters, nieces, ladies from the
church. "Where is the list from last year?
Who did I forget?" Phone calls to the last few
names that come to mind.

My Aunt Jo lives with my Granny in a
large brick home my great grandfather built
for his new bride. Jo holds a tea every year,
usually in April when her flowers bloom
their best, but sometimes later when we can
be there to help.

Silver candelabra darken the rag in
the sink. Silver teaspoons and salad forks
wait their turn. Rugs are beaten. Oriental

colors glow in the sunlight. Lace curtains
pulled back, let the pear tree blooms be
seen though the window. Cut linen, lace
tablecloths, and matching napkins cool on
the refrigerator shelves waiting for the iron.

Hand washed vases filled with water
wait for blooms from the garden. Azaleas,
late blooming daffodils, hydrangeas barely
open, sweet lily of the valley
drape across the back porch table awaiting
their watery assignment. Mantels and
corner cupboard are hand polished. The
breakfront and long tables anticipate their
cue to stand up and display the food that
will come.

Cheese sticks, chicken salad
sandwiches – without crusts, mixed nuts,
delicate pecan balls rolled in powdered
sugar, ladyfingers, and homemade mints,
olive and cream cheese spread on tiny
crusts. Two kinds of punch, one has
pineapple sherbet floating on top.

Sheet cake frosted and waiting.
Slices must be cut just so. All made the
week before by Aunt Jo or Mary, the black
woman who works at the school lunchroom.
She comes in a gray uniform with white
apron to keep the trays full. Later she
washes up all the dishes. She stays in the
kitchen.

The grass was cut and cars moved

across the road to the barn lot. Open the
double doors to the front porch. Clean the
windows at the side step's porch. Flower
baskets sit at the porch edge. A fresh coat
of gray paint went on the floor that spring.

Trays in place, tiny forks, and odd-
shaped spoons sit beside crystal dishes.

"Get dressed, comb your hair." My
shoes hurt my feet already.

"Can I take your wrap? Please come
inside," small talk of the kindest nature.
Southern gentlewomen talk with lots of
"Don't you knows." Violet, the color of old
women is prevalent; blues and pinks, broad
flowered silks and pleated linens, short
jackets. Slim skirts. No pants suits, no
palazzo wide legs or flower child gauze but
hats with netting and gloves past your wrist,
sensible shoes here and there. Unneeded
fur stoles and jewels steal a few glances.
Dyed-to-match shoes, purses and
perfumed hugs that suffocate me in huge
breasts.

They talk as if they haven't seen
each other in years. "Was it only last week?"
"How are the children, where are they living
now?" "It's a shame they are so far away."
And many "Don't you know?"s.

Big sister pours the punch. Cousin
Coral cuts the cake. I give out nuts. "Would
you like some nuts?" Are they through

nibbling?

"May I take your plate, please?" Give them to Mary to wash.

"Smile and be sweet, you will have your own tea one day," smiles Aunt Jo. What I would really like is to take off my shoes, get out of this tight bodiced dress and sticking slip – no air conditioner, lie on the porch swing and float in the air. Listen to bumble bees, chase the cows in the pasture, read comic books, hide among the boxwoods, and watch the goings on.

If I really had my druthers, I'd like to be trim and petite like my other cousins, have long shiny hair that falls down my back and ties up in a pretty bow.

"Behave now and see what needs to be done. Only one hour more and the tea will be over," Momma encourages.

At last, the lingering talkers leave. Pack up the sandwiches in plastic containers. Tinfoil the mints and freeze what can be. Come drink up some punch. I want the sherbet cupful. All the nuts are gone. Lick off the cake plate with pointer finger so daintily. Peel off the dress, kick off the shoes. Jo's tea time is over. Mary smiles at me, "Don't you know?"

Aunt Christine

We called her Sissie, but she was named
after her aunt 'Tine or Christine. She was Sit
to her mother. My mother called her Sister. I
first remember her on the beach in a two
piece bathing suit and a funny straw hat. I
don't remember if it was Cherry Grove or
Myrtle Beach, SC., but she and Uncle Bill had
rented a cottage on the oceanfront.

Her two children were a little older
than I was. They showed me how to make
drip castles and toad houses. Perhaps they
were toe houses because to make them, you
covered up your toes with sand and packed
it down firmly. Then you carefully pulled
your foot out. The mosquito bites and the
sun burns were the worst at their beach – or
maybe it was because I was having so much
fun I didn't notice until it was too late. I'll
never forget the smell of that Noxzema and
vinegar elixir.

Sissie was fond of pedal pushers at a

time women didn't wear slacks in public. A practical woman, pants made sense to her. During those days of pedal pushers, she frequently donned a handkerchief around her head. She wore many bandanna scarves over the years on her head or tied smartly about her neck.

Her Kings Mountain home was a real treat to visit, whether we came to stay overnight or just for dinner. Oriental carpet, needlepoint chairs, floral upholstery, and wood. I remember lots of wood. It was always so elegant and yet, very comfortable.

She was the first person I remember who baked chicken while the South still fried everything. Her meals were so delicious, even though she invented low fat and nutritious menus. The nights we stayed up to play Clue and other board games in her den, we slurped up High C until our mouths turned red from the drink.

There was a wonderful hammock hung in the back yard between two enormous trees. It was 15 feet long, so it held all of us kids. No matter how hard Daddy or Cousin Billy tried to swing us, we clung on and we never fell out.

Often we would load up a picnic lunch, put on our bathing suits, and go to Lake Montonio. The drive seemed like forever. They hadn't built the four-lanes yet. My Dad courted my Mom up near their mountain and I liked to watch it as we drove. I loved the trips and swimming out to the float, treading water and listening to echoes between the pontoons.

Even an unfortunate time at Sissie's is remembered fondly. Somehow, I stepped on glass and shoved a sliver into my heel. She took me up to Uncle Bill's office where he cut out the glass and swathed my heel in purple stuff and bandage. On the way home, we stopped at the fish market and bought swordfish. She grilled it for supper that night. Talk about yummy! I never tasted any better swordfish.

I have to mention the laughs of the home movies. As we sat in the living room, old cartoons and family events flashed on the screen. We paused from the world that was barreling by outside on those lightening bug nights. Years later, my cousin, Bill, put the family films on video so that we can enjoy those same events today, forty plus years later. My daughter and husband never knew Aunts Jo and Maxie, or Uncle Bill. Now we can watch them in living color with all their antics, funny clothes, and expressions.

Aunt Sissie, the school teacher, always had a story about one of her school children. She told us about a little boy she sent to the coat closet to get a tissue because he was continually sniffing during class. "Go back there and find something to fix your runny nose."

He came out with a piece of chalk stuck up each nostril. I guess that stopped the drip for sure! She had that little cackle laugh that made you grin even when you didn't get the joke.

She treated Zerada, her maid, and other black people like they were white people. Uncle Bill couldn't see to drive. He had a man who drove for him and did the handy work about the house. Zerada and her husband, the driver, lived above the garage in a little apartment. Anyway, I got used to seeing African Americans in their kitchen and around the house. Of course, they weren't "black" or African-Americans back then, we called them Negro, Negra or worse. I don't know how the South could have gotten so vile on the matter, but I wasn't afraid of black people after being in Sissie's home.

When Uncle Bill died so many years ago, she went right on living for the family. She finished a porch project and had the living room painted. She said that she and Uncle Bill had decided to do that. She was going to stick with the plan. I thought that widowhood could have been an empty time but loneliness never seemed to be in her life. She filled it with bridge, friends, work, and new ideas. She was a 'steel magnolia,' a term I hadn't heard until the movie, but it fits.

Aunt Sissie got into basketball. She knew the players and their teams and could discuss them. I guessed she did that to be able to have something to talk about with her grandsons. She even had my Mom watching them for a while.

She was always sharp as a tack. Her mind was clear and she grew old gracefully like a Southern butterfly.

Her stockings' seams were always straight. That's when we had seams. Her purse matched her shoes and her lipstick was never a mess.

Just after my husband, Denton, and I married, we went to Mary Jo's Fabric in Gastonia to buy fabric to make slipcovers for our couch. It was a 300 mile drive for us, but I called her to see if she would like to "do lunch" while we were there.

She was 82 at the time. She showed up well dressed and pert as always waiting for us outside the S&W Cafeteria, another Southern staple. I hope I am as agreeable and full of it when I get to be that age.

Last year, at the reunion at Uncle Charles', she was more into the conversation than any one else. She could carry on polite conversation with great-grand kids and their parents. A chuckling cackle always present in her talk. She still dressed like those little store clerk ladies of Montaldo's. She wore dark hose, a handkerchief around her neck and nice pen on her lapel. She had more fun than anyone, because I think she was looking forward – not back when she talked. I think she knew which child was whose brother or sister's offspring and talked with everyone.

She was ahead of her time on downsizing her home and finding a retirement center. She took responsibility for giving away and getting rid of all her "stuff." She sold the house and made a very comfortable new home for herself in Matthews at a retirement center. She died quietly after Christmas a few years back.

Aunt Christine was real special to me. I named my daughter Christine. I will miss Aunt Sissy, but her memories are with me always. She was a jewel of the family crown, the second of eight children, middle sister of three. Whatever life offered her, she took it like a hot knife through butter. I'm so glad I shared the time I did with her. Her spirit continues to roam the South, especially when I hear a little cackle laugh.

Sarah Rhyne

Someone once said that Southern double names, like Mary Lou, Beth Anne, or Emily Dean, have a way of blessing a girl child. Maybe it's because the Southern heart is captured by a double name, like my little sister's, Sarah Rhyne. Today her large brown eyes can tame any contrary horse, quiet a squalling child, and stymie any person from above the Mason-Dixon Line who is not aware of a Southern style total woman. But I'm getting ahead of myself.

It was Christmas Eve, 1960. Over 24 cousins, eight aunts, and uncles with matching spouses had gathered at my grandmother's house to celebrate the season. Being a freshman in high school, I was younger than the cousins who talked about courting and their boyfriends and older than the ones who were about to sneak around to the formal living room and shake and/or open every present under the tree that looked the least bit interesting.

I wandered into the living room with its Louis XVth needlepoint love seats, velveteen tufted wing chairs with matching floor stools, porcelain bric-a-bracs, and the ceiling-high cedar tree decorated with crystals and red bows.

The den was reserved for the smokers and anyone who could stand their company. It was where the boys usually sat to watch ballgames, but this night the house was packed. People were everywhere downstairs. The meal was served, eaten, and cleaned up. Card tables and folding chairs were wiped and packed away. Most of the women were somewhere between the kitchen and the breakfront, cleaning out the last of the dishes and putting away the leftover food. The men gravitated to the breakfast room between the formal dining room and the kitchen. I'm sure there was a flask or two inside a jacket.

Suddenly there was a big "Whoopee!" The laughter quickly spread to the aunts and cousins. Daddy and Momma received the biggest brunt of the exclamations. Word seeped down to me. It seems I was the last to find out that my Momma was pregnant!

I mean there were four years between my big sister and me. She had already graduated from high school and was in college. My brother was six years behind me. I figured they stopped after they got "the boy." But, I was to have another sibling.

###

Daddy literally raised the roof at our house adding two bedrooms and another bath upstairs. The little bundle of joy was due in August. Mom had a series of false labors. So the last time Daddy came on home and left Mom at the hospital 30 miles away. When the phone rang later that night, he kept running into the full- length mirror door trying to get to the kitchen. He was so excited he didn't remember he had closed the door between himself and the kitchen phone.

I now had a little sister. Long dark hair sprouted from the top of a head that more often than not made ugly faces. Mom let Daddy name her and so she became Sarah Rhyne, named after my mother.

I learned how to change diapers, feed her a bottle, and burp her. We all started wearing that diaper-on-our-shoulder because we never knew when we would be called into service. Sarah Rhyne was in the Olympic trials for hurling her milk after feedings. The other favorite thing Sarah Rhyne liked to do was to cry –

unceasingly. Only when we all got into the station wagon and rode over the railroad tracks in town did she finally fall asleep. Riding around town for months after her birth, we discovered neighborhoods we didn't even know about.

I was in high school with a life that became more complicated; then off to college. She grew up quickly. I came home one time to find a large hole at the bottom of the stairs. Brother had talked her into donning a football helmet and riding a cardboard box down the steps. She was fearless.

I'd find baby rabbits, a duckling, and a seagull with a busted wing, a crow, and numerous cats in various forms of kittenhood hanging around our house. Sarah Rhyne could talk a catbird out of a tree. Critters were attracted to her. Neighbors dropped off animals at our house just for her, and because they got tired of them.

She had a longhaired calico cat named Oto (rhymes with low–toe) that thought she was a dog. Oto followed Sarah Rhyne around guarding her like a dog would. She could get that cat to stand on its hind legs, rollover and I half expected it to raise a paw to shake. And don't ever get between that cat and her food bowl after she's heard the sound of a whirring can opener!

I married and was away for a few years. When I came back, I didn't recognize Sarah Rhyne. The little dark haired girl with a great tan, for she browned up good in the summertime, had grown up. Her pug nose had narrowed. Mom tried to keep her hair cut short, but now her hair was long with a bit of a curl. She twirled a baton and marched in parades. Later there was a flute, piccolo, recorder, and marching band spectaculars.

About the time she ran for homecoming queen there began a different kind of parade. Boys began showing up on a regular basis on weekends.

Sarah Rhyne graduated from high school and attended the same college where I taught. We started our friendship all over again. It was fun getting to know my little sister, who was becoming a very attractive and talented woman. We went shopping, horse back riding, shared suppers, and lots of laughter.

Now it's over two decades since college and she still has her trained animals. Today's count is three cats named Melvin, Howard, and Mugsy. Three dogs named Toby, Caboodle, and Junie. The big critters are Harley, named for the bike her husband never got, Meko, a quarter horse and a thoroughbred named Al Capone who answers to Woody. Go figure.

She's still an eye catcher. She owns a pottery business, trains horses in dressage, and teaches riding. Each business in itself could be a full time job. She shows up when we meet for lunch or supper with some startling exclamation. I think people are still charmed by my little sister, but don't let her get her hot Italian side up. (We are not Italian, but she does a good impression.)

When I think about that Christmas Eve 40-some years ago, I'm not surprised by anything she does. She lives up to her double name, Sarah Rhyne, a Southern blessing all its own.

Lap Chores and Other Lessons

We didn't get an allowance when we were young. We earned our money the old fashion way, cleaning our rooms, doing the dishes, and taking out the garbage. We vacuumed the house, dusted all the knick-knacks, and swept off the porch. We mowed the grass and got paid in nickels and quarters, our weekly wage.

In the summer, we washed windows or cars in the neighborhood, and baked and sold cookies. We put on circus shows inspired by the Little Rascals and Our Gang antics. We did magic tricks, hopped dogs through hoops and clowned our way across the garage-stage. But the things that taught me the lessons of life and heritage were lap chores.

Lap chores were sitting with a mess

of green beans, a newspaper, and a bowl in your lap, stringing and snapping those crisp green fingers, or cutting out the bad spots from slicing apples you picked up in the pasture. Lap chores were shelling pecans and walnuts that fell on the ground outside the garage or darning socks, ripping out a seam or hemming a dress, cutting scraps from old clothes or remnants for colorful quilts.

My mother was an excellent lap chore teacher. Wearing a flowered bibbed apron, she'd settle on one of those metal step-stool chairs where the light was good. If cutting, she'd choose a time-worn thin bladed, dark wooden handled knife. If it were sewing, a Sharp needle was threaded and the sewing thread bitten off. (I never learned how to bite off thread, but Momma would raise the string to her mouth and bite off the end in one click of her teeth.)

We'd sit for as long as it took our hands to do the chore. I mainly listened while she talked about the weather or relatives, well and sick. She'd plan a menu, share a recipe, or just sit amid her own private thoughts.

I learned other things from her, too. I never heard Momma cuss or say "No," when asked to bake a dish for the sick or serve on a homeroom committee. She wrapped bandages when there was war in the Congo. She sewed aprons, shawls and baby wraps for the poor. She cooked for the Church Suppers. She served as chair of Girl Scout cookie sales and Band Booster orange sales, filling our garage to the ceiling with stacked boxes. She worked in the snack stand and cookouts for Little League and Halloween Carnivals. She sewed all our clothes right up through high school and then went on to sew for her grandchildren.

Lap chores and chores in general with Daddy took a different angle. We'd head and shell shrimp. Open clams for chowder grinding. We'd stand at a wooden bench, Daddy made for that purpose, and clean a mess of spots or croakers we caught that morning up by the Coast Guard Station. I'd hold the solder as he melted it for some electronic gizmo he was either building or repairing. He never burned my fingers, but the acrid smoke watered my eyes if I got too close. I learned about cold and hot solders. I learned to splice a line and finish the end of a newly cut one. I learned how to tie off a boat the right way.

I never got paid in dimes or quarters for those kinds of chores. What I received was a strong background of doing things right. Daddy said, "Never say anything bad about anyone." "If you're going to do something, do it right the first time." He didn't have to be asked for help by friend or stranger. He was there with his tools, a strong back, and helping hand. After Daddy sold his boat, he hauled it, had it painted, and put in new batteries. I learned to give a hundred percent when asked.

My parents sponsored the first teenage group of Senior Highs for our Church. They attended Republican Block meetings. They made sure we all went to church Sunday morning. They helped us with our homework and established rules. I don't know how different that was from growing up somewhere else. I'd like to think this was peculiar to my parents. Maybe all kids in the South had the same strict tutelage.

Can't say that's true for today. Some kids never learned to head shrimp. Some never knew the importance of being on time. Some never learned to pull a net from the stern of a boat. Many never understood the value of a person's word.

Words like charity, responsibility, and courtesy were practiced, not preached. Maybe lap chores and such weren't just in my home. Maybe it was just the South or growing up with my parents.

I got paid the old fashion way growing up. I'm still collecting the returns.

Peace Making Yeast Bread

We moved into our new house in 1954. It
was the only house my parents ever built. It
had gray asbestos shingles and white trim.
The kitchen had white enamel cabinets with
a drain board sink. Little windows looked
through wooden double garage doors. The
oil heat furnace required a chimney and a
big oil tank out back that I often rode like a
horse. The picture window had a row of
smaller windows below, that pushed out to
allow a breeze to blow through the house.
There were three bedrooms and a bath. My
parent's bedroom had two doors which
allowed entrance and egress for a great
raceway when the grandchildren ran the
circle around the inside. The children
weren't allowed to do that. That room later
became known as the sewing room after

Daddy built more bedrooms and bathroom upstairs. The kitchen had a long bar that stuck out over the enamel cabinets between the kitchen and the dining area. A new gas range guarded one wall. A corner was added specifically for Momma's corner cupboard in the dining room, which later became more living room, when Daddy took in one side of the garage for the paneled dining room and inside laundry room.

When everything was moved in and settled, Granny came to visit. Granny lived on a big farm 300 miles away. I visited her on Christmas and holidays. I went to stay a few weeks every summer. She had a big brick home built before the War Between the States. It had a long porch wrapping around two sides of the house and a pantry off the breakfast room. I learned to make butter in a glass churn with a wooden paddle. I learned to use the sewing machine. I learned about cooking fresh vegetables, especially how to cook okra without making it slimy and baking home made bread during those visits.

Granny wasn't the kind of grandmother I am today. I retired early from my career. I live on a boat part of the year. Blue jeans and shorts are every day clothes for me. My Granny wore flowered shirtwaist dresses with thin matching cloth belts. She wound her long hair into a bun at the back of her head and held it there with combs and hairpins. She rolled her stockings above her knees with garters and wore sensible leather shoes. Her wire-rimmed glasses were smudged and she left her teeth on the nightstand when she went to bed.

My grandfather died when Momma was two years old. Granny single-handedly put all her eight children through college. She demanded a hard day's work from her children. It was no wonder they nicknamed her Turnip behind her back. Getting extra spending money from her was like trying to get blood from a turnip.

When Granny came to visit, I guess she expected to be a part of the working family at my Momma and Daddy's home. We took her to our favorite seafood restaurant, Captain Tony's Sanitary Restaurant, where we took all our guests. We went to the beach and to historical sights. We took her to New Bern where they had opened the Tryon Palace. They hollered at her for sitting on one of the chairs, when she got tired. We didn't go back there for a long time.

Then we just fell back into our regular daily routine. Momma did all the cooking. We girls washed the dishes and did the rest of the chores.

The summer breeze blew through the house. We thought Granny would sit and enjoy being there with us. Well, I don't remember the exact words of the argument but I remember it was loud. I had never heard my Granny get angry! She wanted something to do around the house. Momma didn't want her to do anything. Granny got so mad she went to her room and slammed the door. Momma cried.

I went outside to play. When I came back, Granny was making bread. She made bread every day after that. There is something cathartic about making yeast bread. While stirring and kneading bread, anger, fear, frustration, and stress work out with harmless force. Granny tried every recipe in the *Better Homes and Garden Cookbook.* When she finished that cookbook, she started another one.

Our family ate freshly baked bread every day as long as she stayed. She would flour the counter and knead the dough tenderly. She used slow strong motions that worked the flour and butter, frothy yeast and salt together. Sometimes she'd make it into stickies, brushing it with melted butter, adding cinnamon and sugar. Sometimes she'd halve the dough, roll it into long rectangles, and fold into loaves, easing them gently into loaf pans. Other times she would "gob" off little pieces. Like a magician, she'd make tiny balls appear from nowhere as she made cloverleaf dinner rolls. The plain yeast breads were my favorites. Watching her make those wonderful breads was a real treat.

Sometimes she'd let me help. I often thought her movements were close to a mother tenderly lifting her child to bed as she eased newly shaped dough into pans.

One day she made bread that just didn't taste right. The recipe called it Amadama bread. Maybe we weren't used to the strong flavors of the ingredients. Maybe it was a sad loaf, which happens sometimes. We joked about that Amadama bread with its funny taste, texture, and look.

I never heard my mother and grandmother argue again. My Granny died many years ago. Daddy and Momma died recently. My Momma enjoyed her first great grandchild for two years before she died. In my retirement, I have started making bread again. The motion of heating the milk, stirring yeast into a bit of warm water with a pinch of sugar is inborn. When a friend comes to visit, they leave with a loaf of bread or dinner rolls. When I make bread with my granddaughter, she sits on the kitchen counter watching me knead the dough or plays with a gob of dough. I make loaves and rolls, but my stickies need more practice. My Momma came to eat with us one time my granddaughter visited. When Momma came to dinner she ate my yeast bread and we talked about the summer long ago of the Amadama bread. I believe bread making, like saying grace, going to church and brushing your teeth, needs to be taught in every home. Needing (kneading) bread helps to shape and heal a family.

(The first picture of this story is my grandmother, Coral Rhyne. She's holding Sarah Rhyne Kale. The above picture is the author and her granddaughter making bread.)

Pony Penning

Many island communities along the coast rounded up their ponies every year. It began as a way to simply thin the herds but has grown into a tourist attraction and opportunity for fundraising.

I was just a horse crazy girl in an old T-shirt, cowboy boots, and dungarees. At the age of seven or eight a girl finds out if, she is horse crazy or not and unfortunately all the girls in my family leaned towards favoring horses much to my father's dismay. I overheard him tell someone one time that he had enough shoveling up behind a horse for his lifetime. His father was a horse trader.

Someone mentioned ponies and I begged to go down to the end of the island. A big crowd gathered there. Fish and hushpuppies popped in the deep vats of hot grease. Skinny riders sat on lean horses, which chomped lather onto their bits. Riders and boaters swam the ponies across the sound. Tourists came from all over to watch the sights, to eat fried seafood, and take pictures. I heard about a frightened mare struggling in the surf. A boater reached down to hold up her head, some photographer had the picture in the local paper.

The stallions were separated from the herd; the old mares let loose. A baby horse is kicked in the neck. A wide blood dripping gap in its neck spoiled the fun for onlookers. It was destroyed out of sight.

Terrified horses raced around the pen. A rope thrown and a neck caught. The pony pulled to the edge, trembled beneath human hands. Bids called through the dust; a loose horse caught. The sun dried to salt the water on the shaggy coats. Drinking water for the ponies brought into the pen.

The crowd thinned at the pen, as the meals began selling. Grease soaked paper plates loaded with food, covered with tissue. The smell of hot grease choked the heat and dust in the air. Bottled cold drinks provided to wash it down. A wrangler hitched up his belt and loosened the cinch for his own horse.

My daddy knew a man on a horse. Before I could holler, "Whoopee," I was lifted

up to sit in front of him, on the saddle. I
have never been so high. I forgot the
bleeding colt and the bright sun overhead. I
forgot my hunger and thirst. I only
remembered the horse's first step and the
feeling of my first horse beneath me.

On the long ride home, I imagine a
having my own horse. When I got older, I
did have a house and acreage. I almost got
a horse, but I was accepted into the
doctorial program at the University of
Florida. That was the choice I made, an
education over a horse and I never looked
back.

Log Cabin Quilts

Granny sits in the chair by the window. There's good light. Her basket of cloth scraps sits on the floor, her tiny sharp scissors slice through the fabric. She wears a cobbler apron with big pockets, which hold her quilt patterns, threads, scissors, and thimble. She uses pasteboard patterns to cut the different shaped pieces.

She forms the design in her mind knowing how it will look. Sometimes the pattern looks like an Aztec temple. Those "logs" appear to climb from larger to smaller. Other times there is a log cabin shape as four pyramids connect to build a larger square. It all depends on which color she uses where. She uses scraps of cloth left over from sewing a coat, a skirt, a dress, or a blouse.

She has baskets of cotton gingham, worsted, herringbone woolens, and plaids. The cotton florals are spring like, delicate and airy. I see pieces of a summer skirt and blouse, aprons scraps, baby, and doll clothes.

The velveteen scraps are rich, soft luxuriant to touch and see. I run my hands over them feeling the velveteen pile break beneath my fingers. I imagine the robes of royalty beneath my hands. These same fabrics made our Christmas stockings when we were children. Sequins and beaded pearls form reindeer, Christmas trees, and stars on a dark field of velveteen. Sequins sewed individually across the cuff spelled my name. A pearl or bead held down each sequin. Each stocking was hand stitched as each family grew another child or spouse. Sometimes homemade tatting or lace trimmed the cuff of the velveteen stockings. I see my family's Christmas stocking colors in my own velveteen quilt.

The wools are scruffy, rough to touch. Some have larger weave, which make lumpy rectangles on the quilt. Some are smoother with a fuzzy hand, somber plaids for winter spreads. I have a heavy wool log cabin quilt stored in the guest bedroom cedar chest for cold winter nights. It must be over 80 years old. It is made of plaid, tweed, and herringbone wool pieces. Tiny stitches sewn long ago break apart, form jagged tooth-like pulls among the wool and lining. The weave differs on each piece of rectangle. It is made up of old coats torn apart and remade for the next younger child, skirt hems from when the hemlines rose from the ankles to below the knee. The center square is velvet sometimes.

There is a large basket of empty spools under the hallway steps. We children pull them out on quiet nights and build monster castles on the floor at her feet as she stitches. We stack the thin and fat wooden spools across the room in straight lines between her feet and across the rag rug before the hearth. In the summer, a fan blows across the floor stirring a breeze, which often topples the castles before their time. During the winter, hickory wood crackles in the den fireplace warming our faces as we crouch on the floor. Bits of scraps are draped across the roofs, which lean under the weight.

Granny collects cloth scraps in her basket all year for her quilts. Here are pieces of a winter coat. There a wool scrap of a skirt my mother wore to church. I remember it because during the sermon I would rest my head in her lap and outline the design with my finger. There are scraps of wool trousers worn thin from too many sittings. The good wool cut apart and held back for a quilt. I can look over a quilt and see the people who wore them when the scraps were whole.

Granny remembers them as she sits, cuts, and pieces the bits of cloth together. She sees wars, church suppers, presidents, grocery store prices, friends, and family. She sees a husband who died too soon.

She sees her mother who taught her to piece scraps together. She slices through a green wool Army uniform and remembers a son who returned wounded while somewhere else another woman sews together wool uniform bits from a son who never came home.

I don't know what makes a woman choose a particular design; Granny uses the log cabin pattern a lot.

I've heard the center square is like the heart of the home. The strips of fabric get larger working out from the center square and then begin to shrink toward the small square heart. A woman at the fabric store corrected me one day when I told her about my quilts. She said, "The log cabin design is not really quilting – more like piece work." Her cutting remarks don't bother me.

I love the quilts my Granny made. In later years, she made each daughter or granddaughter a velveteen quilt as a wedding gift. My quilt outlasted my first marriage. My wedding quilt is primarily rose with aqua and blue logs. My mother's has royal blue logs.

I bring out my quilts when I am cold, to shake off the winter winds and doldrums. When I outline the edge of a square with my finger, I feel I am connecting with the woman who stitched it over a half century ago. I can feel her strength and courage, her sadness and joy among the stitches. I remember days of watching her thread the needle, biting off the thread end, and rolling a knot at the end with two fingers.

Her hands held the edges together as she stitched not only cloth and thread but also a thought and a memory for me. My quilts will go to my daughter and then to her daughter after we are gone. With them, I give not only pieced scraps of fabric but also bits of memories from generations of decent women.

Miss America

Most little girls in the 1950s and 1960's sat,
once a year, with their whole family in front
of the only one black and white television in
the house, cheering their favorite girl to the
pinnacle of success: the Miss America crown.
The televised event preceded by daily
coverage in newspapers and national
magazines. Gorgeous gowns, discrete
bathing suit shots, talent competitions, and
family histories were newsworthy.

The young women looked alike and
yet they were all different. Sweet, intelligent,
speakers on their feet, they enchanted Burt
Parks and America with their candid
remarks. We watched every state and "Owah"
or "Ah"ed each girl as she walked across the
stage and stood in a pre-marked spot, the
state printed across her satin ribbon
bandeau and the bottom of our screen.

The best ten were named to the
delight and smiles of well wishers. A lot of
hugging followed. You already knew a
couple of the finalists, because of the point
system totals published during the previous
week.

By the time the first of the ten took her bathing suit stroll across the stage, we were betting on who would win. Television polls that night proved everyone in the country was interested in the next Miss America. Little girls hoped and wished they were up there.

During the talent competitions, my Momma and Daddy would evaluate our own talents as we danced across the floor, twirled batons, did summersaults, or sang at the top of our lungs. We glided across the room with a book balanced on our heads, or rather falling, and again took our seat as the final three and Miss Congeniality was announced. There was an abundance of hope and excitement in the final minutes as Burt Parks sang his song and the newly crowned and robed Miss America took the stage, staggering under the load of her crown, responsibility, and prizes. Her thrill went with me as I brushed my teeth and slept, dreaming about sparkling crowns and velveteen robes, high heels, smiling turns, with adoring fans.

Beauty contests today take a back seat to Monday Night football, reality shows, violent or sex-filled programming, cartoons, and sitcoms. I don't even know when we have a new Miss America until after the fact. It's good that multi-racial and handicapped

women can now win. A new role of the
titleholder is to tout their particular cause.

Formerly, winners went into stage
performances or sold appliances. Now they
make records, model beguiling lingerie, or
speak candidly about their thoughts.

Times in deed have changed. The
murder of a small girl, a beauty competition
winner, brought more attention to the earlier
stages of this final step. The makeup,
clothes, and advanced talents on these
miniature women are ridiculous when you
watch their home videos or spy competition
winners in local papers.

I look into the eyes of a smiling
munchkin with teased and fluffed hair,
costumed in sequins, and eyes made up like
Jackie Gleason's Maybelline women and
wonder if this is what she really wants or
what her mother wants. I wonder if she ever
played in mud, skinned her knees on roller
skates, and ran shouting about the house
like a banshee just because she wanted to do
it. Their perfect smile and poise seems as
plastic as the topless dancer's, jolting across
the dark barroom stage.

Competitions have been marred with
bad publicity, bribes, slander, and vulgarity.
I think back to those nights on the couch in
our living room when I could just about bust
with pride for the new Miss America. The

show, if it is televised, now a production of color, lights, choreography, minuscule bathing suits, sensuality – a money and glamour promotion. Do little girls go to bed after watching the show, hoping that she could be the one or is it like any other program she watches? We used to beam with joy for the new Miss America because it meant hope for America that something good and wholesome was representing us all over the world.

What happened to that feeling?

Drive-In Movies

We started the preparation on Thursday.
Momma got out the meat grinder, clamped it
onto the kitchen counter, and ran though it a
can of Spam, and a jar of pickles. The
mixture came out into a pie plate resting on
the counter. A bowl on a metal chair beneath
the grinder caught any escaping juice. She
added mayonnaise to the mixture and placed
it into a plastic container she bought at a
Tupperware party. If she were in the mood
for pimento cheese, a quick wash in the
enamel dishpan, always filled with tepid
water in the sink made it ready to use again.

   We'd turn huge chunks of cheese and
whole pimentos into slushy sandwich filler,
also held together by the Kraft spread of
choice.

   She bought big jars of assorted
pickles with tiny onions in the bottom under
pickled cauliflower, peppers, and whole
pickles. On Friday afternoon, she made
deviled eggs, brownies, or oatmeal cookies
and spread either of the two fillings between
soft white bread. The sandwiches snapped
shut and burped in more Tupperware. Daddy

came home from work and we took our baths. Sometimes we kids wore our pajamas, other times we pulled on clean clothes. We were rubbed down with mosquito repellant, our hair combed into place, and we climbed into the back seat of our 1949 Oldsmobile.

Along with the children, there would be a hamper of good things to eat. Momma also packed a jug of Kool-Aid, cups and damp wash cloths for cleaning up spills and messy hands.

We arrived at the drive-in just before dark. Sometimes Daddy would jokingly ask one of us to duck down under a blanket to keep the total below three dollars, but we never did. After our heads were counted and Daddy paid the gatekeeper, we bounced our way over the rutted lane to a center spot on a hill. He angled the car on a bump so we could see the screen, as we sat in the back seat.

While the snack shack glowed in the early evening darkness, we unwrapped our sandwiches, eggs, pickles, and poured drinks.

Daddy would hook the speaker on the window leaving a small crack so mosquitoes would have to work harder to find our fresh meat. We would balance our meal on small laps, careful not to tip our drink cups, and watch the first cartoon dance

across the screen. (Cars didn't have cup
holders back then.)

An elf would entertain us by eating
one of everything available at the snack
shack: hotdogs with relish, popcorn, ice
cream, fries, cold drinks, candy bars. The elf
would lick his fingers, with enthusiasm, after
each treat. The newsreel followed with clips
of the Korean War, Eisenhower waving to the
troops, and French fashions. Sometimes we
saw the Queen of England or Pope. News
clips at the movies were a way people kept
informed about world events during the early
1950's. Then coming features' previews with
rapturous heroines, clutched by handsome
heroes, or white hatted cowboys galloped
across the screen to rescue stagecoach with
passengers screaming from the windows,
shootouts, and grim faced detectives.

By this time, one of us had to go to
the bathroom and Daddy or Momma would
take our hand and lead us off into the dark.
Then there would be cartoons. "Tom and
Jerry" were my favorites, Elmer Fudd and
Bugs Bunny, Sylvester and Tweety Bird
saying, "I t'ought I taw a putty tat!" If we
were lucky, we saw two cartoons.

Then the main feature would begin
with music and dancing or it might be a
cowboy flick or detective drama – usually
Momma liked the musicals but Dad went for

the cowboys. We didn't care; it was a night out at the drive-in. We sat, our backs straight in the back seat; our heads propped back, our "feet off the seat." We'd munch our brownies and sip Kool-Aid.

Occasionally one of us would put a foot across another and a spat would begin, stopped by Daddy who would grab the closest one and give us a yank.

Most times, we were awake from the first pass of the mosquito fog truck to the last, "That's All Folks!" Dad would place the microphone back on the stand, roll up the window, and watch the traffic slowly make their way out the exit. He didn't start the car until we could get out without a long wait.

When I was a single parent, another mother and I would pile our kids into a car, pack pre-cooked popcorn, fast food, candy bars, or soft drinks to take in a drive-in double feature. Drive-ins were cheap enjoyable entertainment.

I haven't seen a working drive-in in quite a while. During the 1970's, they became flea markets on weekends or were bull-dozed to become shopping centers or golf driving ranges. Too bad.

Drive-ins were a special evening with my family and many other Southerners.

Painting Picket Fences

Have you ever had the opportunity to paint a picket fence in the heat of the summer, on an airless morning, when all the mosquitoes and gnats that haven't eaten since you disappeared the night before, reappear? The itchy grass tickles your ankles better aggravating the experience. I dreaded the first few weeks of my 5th grade summer. It became the first of many summers that the picket fence needed painting.

You see, Momma wanted a picket fence but my daddy didn't want to have to paint it. My parents made a decision, that if it were to be, then the kids could do the painting and Momma could have the fence after all.

We got most of the pickets from my grandmother's house. Fortunately, for the hired man, Granny had decided she no longer wanted the white pickets and replaced it with black wrought iron. We loaded all the white daggers into the trailer on one of our Easter visits and came home to a couple of weekends of post hole digging and strung string eyeing and hammering the pickets on boards held up by four by fours planted ten feet apart.

Not even time to have a good sword fight with the spikes before they were all lined up, taunting the neighbor's dogs to lift a leg to them.

Momma saved coupons from All Bran box lids for months to buy the dozen or more red rose bushes, advertised on the back of the cereal box. They were mail ordered and planted at each post, eventually winding themselves in and out of the pickets. The grocer must have thought we were a constipated family for all the boxes we consumed that spring.

The red roses were pretty. We always supplied a plate full of roses each year to church to share with other people on Mother's Day and Father's Day. Down South, we wore red roses to symbolize our Momma or Daddy was living. Someone else always brought a plate of white or yellow ones to indicate a parent was dead.

But, those rose bushes didn't completely hide that fence; it had to be painted every year or so. My big sister and I got the job first. She had her own way and time of doing it. She slept late and was an "artist." So, I let her do her own thing.

I'd rather have been anywhere than sitting on a little chair out in the yard -- first cutting the weeds that were growing up under the pikes, going back a second time to the same spot to paint the back with the long rail and post supports. Then going back to the same spot again and paint the front of the fence and sides of each picket, which is a lot easier because you don't have as much to do. The sides have just been done and all you have, finally is the face of the fence.

What I decided in the initial bargaining for the job was do 10 feet or one section of that fence a day. Any more and the sun would be directly overhead and too hot to work.

So every morning for what seemed like three weeks I was out at 7AM wearing old clothes saved for floundering and grunge work. The tennis shoes showed my toes and when not in use hung by the back door. I found a hat to keep the gnats out of my hair. I wished it had earflaps to keep them from buzzing inside my ears. Gloves were important because without them, blisters popped up in a matter of minutes, as clippers sliced away, beneath the pickets, at the grass.

Sometimes my girlfriend next door came out and sat with me while I hacked and painted. She had lots of boyfriends, we talked school stuff, and the time seemed to go a faster. One thing for sure was if my friend came out, not to slap the paint on the pickets, so it splattered on her. I didn't mind getting it on my hands and on the brush handle, but under no circumstance was I to paint my girlfriend. I can remember a time or two my big sister painted opposite me on the other side. Maybe I splattered a little on her.

The big buckets of white paint came with the syrupy sticky pour stains down the sides because I certainly didn't make that mess. The can of paint sat in the grass beside me and after the grass and rose bushes had been pushed out of the way, I'd pop off the lid and stir the thick white mixture. Sort of looked like ice cream just before it begins to harden, thick and white.

If I concentrate, I can smell it to this day. The brush became a part of my hand. It was a big heavy wide brush with black bristles, which every now and then shed onto the fence or the bucket, becoming part of my artwork. You see I figured the wider the brush the fewer strokes I'd have to make.

I could paint with either my right or my left hand. That brush got heavy at times.

It barely fit inside the edge of that old paint bucket, but it wasn't so big as to touch the sides of the can. It made a slapping sound as I painted.

Sometimes I'd just sit, splat and daydream while I painted. Being in the sixth grade, I figured I had lived half my life in school and with six more to go I figured I'd be in school my whole life. I'd never get out. Sometimes I'd think about what books I was reading or some times Momma had promised to take us to the beach if we were good. I'd think about that. Painting is no easy chore.

I still went to double features at the movies. They were called Saturday matinees and I'd run through what was happening in the last serial. Usually the hero or heroine was left hanging off a building or tied on a train track or wild horses were bearing down on them.

Looking back, painting fences didn't seem so bad. I learned to finish a job I promised to do. I learned to poke little holes in the rim of a paint can to let the excess paint flow back into the can. I learned how important it was to clean up after a job, including washing out your brushes. I guess that fence stood between me being a kid with time on my hands and growing up with responsibilities.

As years went by, I liked seeing the rose bushes growing between the pickets of that fence. I don't know who painted the fence after I felt home. Daddy knocked down the fence when we all left home. He replaced it with a split rail fence that aged with the house. I guess picket fence painting wasn't a bad experience, but Lord-a-mercy, how I hated painting that picket fence back then.

The Pasteboard Valentines Box

One of the traditions in our family every Valentine's Day was making the Valentine's Day box. Usually a few weeks before the red heart day, Daddy would take an old shoe or napkin box, any good sized pasteboard box that was heading for the trash, and cut a large slit in the side. He would scrawl, "Do Not Open Until Valentine's Day" on the side. Sometimes my big sister or I would get to draw big red hearts in crayon or paste on construction paper gaudiness.

I hadn't started first grade yet and Patty came home every day with stories that excited me about going to school next year. She showed me how they did "art work." During the next few days we sequestered ourselves in our room or at the kitchen counter with glitter, paper doilies, construction paper and magazines, from which we cut out roses or hugging couple pictures. She showed me how to stay within the lines and make pretty things for our parents. The rubber tipped glue bottle smeared yellow syrup across the paper on which we pressed cutouts or glitter.

We didn't have today's polite white Elmer's which dries clearly, almost on command. We'd have hands and hair full of glitter, ribbons tangled on the table, bits of lace and smiles in our hearts as we diligently worked on those masterpieces.

Store bought cards weren't easy to come by back then. Besides that was cheating and Hallmark didn't have the sense of humor it has now.

Comes the favored day and we would all sit in excitement around the enamel, pull-out sided kitchen table. I liked to feel the cool white tabletop with its dark blue painted edges. There was a drawer between its legs and the leaves would slide up under one another if we needed to make it smaller. We sat with our chins on the cool tabletop eagerly waiting for Daddy to pull the cards, one at a time, from the box.

He would present the recipient with their card and then everyone would hear the love or laughter revealed. I remember the first time I heard, "Roses are red, violets are blue, your feet stink and so do you!" Momma snorted and glared at Daddy's joke of a card. There was also a lot of love in those carefully made cards.

We would spread out all the cards on the table. Some had to be delivered to homes along the street. We sneaked over, laid the card on the doorstep, rang the doorbell, and ran away. No one wanted to be caught, giving a Valentine. It was sort of like a reverse Halloween.

I had a special drawer where I kept all the cards of my lifetime. I emptied it when we sold my parents' house many years later. The big wide drawer was stale with old year and autograph picture books from elementary school, a wedding shower register, and baby cards with birth and growth measurements charted diligently.

I pulled the drawer from its place and swept the collection into a trash bag along with the glitter, lace, and ribbons. Paper browned from the years of storage and silverfish scuttled across the bottom. Out fell the memories of love from those earlier years. As I toted the black plastic bag of trash down the steps to the garbage can, I remembered my five-year-old child's excitement over my first Valentine card, the flush of excitement of family love, and the joys of growing up surrounded by my family's love.

My parents made marriage and family life look so easy.

The Oyster Can Vacations

Daddy gathered us all around the table, probably on the night after we slurped down hot bowls of oyster stew with crumbly cornbread. He took a screwdriver and cut a slit along the top of the quart oyster can lid, and then emptied all the change from his pockets into the can. "When we fill this up we can go to Florida!"

Now this was before Disney thought of a World in Florida, but there were things we read about that sounded wonderful! Every week we would add change from the groceries, a dollar bill that came in a birthday card with several others, and quarters found behind the cushions of the couch. We kept our earned and gift money in our own banks, but this was the family Vacation Oyster Can.

The can's money would pay for our gas, the motel, and food along the way. We felt proud to add a dime or more when we felt generous. Frequently, my sister, brother, and I were caught shaking the can or peering into the slit of a hole. As the weeks went by, the can got heavier and it made a louder jingle. Dollar bills would flip out a corner occasionally, like a lost wave.

In preparation for the trip, we ordered books, tourist guides, and maps from wherever you ordered those things. The whole family spent evenings reading about the glass bottom boats, St. Augustine's old fort, the swimming mermaids, and the Everglades with its alligators.

My brother was barely five years old. That made me 10, or 11, my sister was fourteen. We planned our trip criss-crossing South Carolina, Georgia, and Florida. There were no super highways built yet.

School let out for the summer and we carried all our things outside. Daddy's job was packing up the car. Our green station wagon had striped plastic seats, and a fold down bench in the back where we could stretch out to sleep or play games.

There was a cooler packed with luncheon meats, pickles, condiments, juice, and milk for the breakfast cereal. We didn't have the fast food restaurants or many choices of motels then. In fact, Momma and Daddy would insist on seeing the room before we unloaded. She would spend the first 30 minutes scrubbing out the tub and toilet and cleaning the room before they would let us out of the car. We even brought our own soap and shampoo.

We'd unload the car, bringing in the suitcases. I had a little brown one with stripes running around the side in beige and tan. I liked snapping it shut and open. It had a satisfying click.

"Don't sit on the motel bedspreads," Momma would tell us. We pulled back the covers lying on the cool sheets and stare at the ceiling cobwebs dancing with each pass of the hotel room fan. Sometimes, we colored in our coloring books.

If a motel had a television, we paid a quarter to watch it for an hour before it shut itself off. Many times, we never saw the end of the show before it shut off. More a real thrill, once Daddy let us put a quarter in the magic fingers vibrating bed machine. We all jumped aboard and rode until it quit bucking, laughing at all the fun.

After checking out the room, we would drive down the road and pull over, most times in a shady spot. We'd place paper plates, plastic forks, and cooler on the folded down back door of the car. Dad set up a folding wooden table that he built where he set the Coleman stove. He'd pump up the pressure and cook corn beef hash, beans or grill sandwiches or hotdogs. Sometimes he'd cook eggs and bacon for us to chomp down before the mosquitoes drove us into the car and back to our room.

Daddy would wipe out the frying pan and store it in a brown paper sack. Mom would wash dirty dishes in the bathroom sink when we got back to the motel. Cooking our own foods, on the side of the road, was an acceptable routine during our trips.

Our first oyster can vacation ended in disaster when little brother got terribly sick. We cut the trip short to get him back to an asthma specialist for testing. Wouldn't you know, he was allergic to chenille bedspreads, the bedspread of choice at 1950's motels.

I still had time to collect souvenirs. I got a couple of new charms for my silver charm bracelet: an alligator and a tiny crate of oranges dangled where once only a horse and an engagement ring in a small box hung.

We went to Canada one year, Disney Land in California another. We camped in the North Carolina Great Smoky Mountains. We rented a tent camper or sought out the starred motels in guidebooks. We ate at a real Mexican food restaurant in El Paso; saw the outdoor dramas of the "Lost Colony" and "Unto These Hills." We swam in a heated pool in New Brunswick and raced lobsters down the hall of our efficiency unit before we boiled them for supper. We watched water run uphill at the Bay of Fundy.

We played alphabet sign games and license plate bingo. Mom bought board games and we divided into teams, the right side of the car against the left side.

That oyster can funded dreams. I remember those trips as I travel today. Sometimes I criss-cross the same roads we traveled 50 years ago. There are four or more lanes now, filled with 18-wheelers, SUVs, soccer mom vans and raging drivers.

Daddy used to politely honk twice to let the car ahead know he was planning to pass. Now a blinking turn light indicates intent to merge in front of you, no asking permission.

The trips of my youth rush back comforting me, now as I travel. I book rooms by internet and know the bed will be comfortable -- and they'll fix me a free breakfast. I can ask to have a little refrigerator in the room.

They provide irons and ironing boards, night lights, laundry service, bottled water, a remote for a colored television and movie rentals, more than I'd ever watch. A clock radio beams the time out to me if I wake in the night. A quieter heat/air conditioning unit is programmed to a comfortable temperature and the drone blanks out the noise of a late arriving neighbor.

At times, it seems plastic or artificial, compared to the trips of my youth. Maybe it's a yearning for long ago. Maybe the change bucket I keep by the back door should be called the "vacation bucket." Full to the brim, it would barely cover the cost of two day's meals. I've been emptying it at the grocery store where it pays for a week's groceries, not much fun there.

That old oyster can guaranteed excitement and kept promises.

Clam Bakes

I remember a Massachusetts clambake when we all gathered on the shore. A 55-gallon barrel held stones heated by huge chunks of burning wood. When the stones were red-hot, the cooks moved fast. In went lobsters, clams, seaweed, net bags of chicken and hotdogs, followed by corn in the husk, and more seaweed. Gallons of water were added last. They yanked a canvas tarpaulin over the top as ropes were wrapped quickly around and tied down. Steam rose, forcing the mushrooming canvas to struggle against the bindings. Then we waited as it all cooked.

Football games, fishing, talking, and playing jokes on old friends continued until we got the word that it was ready. The food was piled, dumped, and scooped on boards held up by sawhorses. The eager crowd stood in line filling their plates. I forget their faces and only remember the ballooning steam-filled tarpaulin over the barrel of wonderful tasting food.

Years later, Momma and Daddy modified the clambake to fit our family. A five-gallon pot is placed on the stovetop. Freshly scrubbed cherry stone clams line the bottom. Irish potatoes, sweet potatoes, shucked corn on the cob, hot dogs, chicken breasts and two cups of water fill the pot. Don't lift the lid before it's done. We wait telling stories of school, work, and family.

We'd scoop out the food in separate bowls and carry it to the screened-in porch outside. "Someone, bring out the potato salad, slaw, ketchup, relish and butter." "I'm bringing pineapple cake, blueberry cream cheese pie. Y'all help with the sweet tea, colas, beer and ice cubes, plastic cups, and heavy divided paper plates, napkins and forks." There were enough hands to tray it all out.

While eating we continued to tell tales of our family. Mind pictures snap as children and grandchildren, preteens without dates, dive into the food. Later clambakes include the grandchildren as grownups with their new boyfriends or spouses. "Put your empty shells and bones in this bucket." "Anyone need anything. I'm going into the house."

Neighbors and friends were invited. Clambakes were special, a never forgotten steamy balm of memories, aching to share the Kale family -- that is now disappearing.

The Christmas Tree Hunt

We never sought glaring lights and canned music of roadside tree lots. Nor did a flannel dressed attendant shouldering trimming saw and bailing string help us. We went on real Christmas tree hunts with my family, down into the pasture climbing over fences watching out for moody cows.

Christmas baking and package wrapping completed, it was time to find our tree. Put on the mittens and headgear. "Place a hankie in your pocket for a runny nose." "Wear the old coat. You don't want to tear your good one on the barbed wire fence." We bundled in layers of clothes and the excitement of the season, holding hands, trudging through the woods.

Mom, Dad with an axe in his hand, Sister, and I, head out. Down into the pasture, hiking together through the gate, hopping over fallen logs. Dad places the axe handle through the chain link fence so we can climb over without being snagged. Carefully climbing up and over, we stand safely on the other side. He places his toe in the hole between the links and hops after us. We change pastures, jumping down off the stone wall. "Crunch," into the leaf covered ground below. We blow moisture, like smoke into the frosty air. Giggling along, we sing Christmas carols accompanied by Daddy's whistle. My father had a wonderful whistle.

The air smells clean and somewhere a hickory fire burns, sending the smell of its smoke our way. A cow calls her new calf close, avoiding the afternoon intruders in her pasture.

In the distance, cars climb a nearby hill, swishing by on their journey home. Holly trees, pecan, and the old black walnut trees stand silently. They seem to watch our progress as we near the cedar grove. Tall, green, pungent sentinels stand at attention directing our gaze upward toward their lofty tops.

It has to fit in the room by the fireplace. There has to be a strong center spire on which to place the silver haired angel. Mom and Dad eye the symmetry. It will stand tall, under its Christmas burden, mantled with colored lights, crystals from broken chandeliers, red velveteen bows, and satin balls. Grandchildren's crude homemade cookie cutter-like artwork hang with pride, tweaking memories.

The tree will be the centerpiece for our Christmas Eve and Christmas Day festivities. The tree's limbs will finger tinsel icicles and strings of glass beads. This tree will be a symbol for this year's celebration. It will greet visitors who shake with the cold as they come through the door. It will provide fragrance throughout the house.

We find the perfect tree. Daddy stands back to see which way to make it fall. We don't want to lose a branch on its descent. Sister and I hold Momma's hand as he strikes the first blow. Five cuts. It falls gracefully. We carefully bind up the limbs for the trip home.

We sing our arrival to the back door. The base and bottom, low hanging limbs are trimmed with a saw. A bucket of water gives it an all-night bath. Oh, look there's a bird's nest among the branches. Hot chocolate awaits us as we peel off our coats and hats.

The next morning we decorate the tree. Boxes of Christmas decorations stand

in the hallway. The cedar branches prick
fingers but the sales lot fir can not compare.
Christmas is coming and we hunted and
found the best tree ever or, at least until
next year.

Shopping and Going to Town

Mothers, grandmothers, and aunts taught shopping to young girls at an early age. It was fine-tuned as teenagers, and garnished as adults.

There were several kinds of shopping in North Carolina during the 1950's. If Momma needed milk, crackers, or a few canned goods, I walked a couple of blocks up to Freeman's Store. It was located on North 20th Street. The single long room with wooden floors and a worn counter on one side served the needs of the community. A wood stove heated the store in the winter. A meat counter in back provided fresh cuts of meat.

Mr. Charles Freeman walked up and down the length of the counter gathering my needs from the wall-mounted shelves behind him, as I recited the list. If I needed ground beef, he stepped to the back and pulled a beef chunk out of the glass case. I watched him grind it. He wrapped it in a white waxed paper and tied it with a string. He stacked everything into a cardboard box, a leftover from stocking his shelves. He did all the calculations in his head and I paid with dollar bills and change.

Since the store ads appeared in Thursday evening's paper, my Momma and I

shopped on Friday. If we go to town, I have
to change clothes. I can't wear jeans to town.
Slacks aren't even acceptable, nor hair
curlers. (Momma didn't own a pair of jeans.
She always wore a dress until polyester knits
came out in the late 1960's. Then she wore
slacks.) At the grocery store, they piled your
groceries in an empty box or brown paper
bags.

Sometimes Momma drove me to
town for the movie on Saturday. When I got
out of the movie, I ambled into downtown
shops with my sister or a friend. We usually
visited every store on the four blocks of
Arendell Street, both sides of the railroad
track, and ended up at Matthew's Drug
Store. They had a free phone for people to
call a taxi or home for a ride. Sometimes I
walked home and other times I called home.

There was a dime store downtown.
(Today it's the Chamber of Commerce.) The
floors creaked when I walked in. It smelled
like popped corn and cotton candy. An ice
cream freezer bar sat in the front, near hair
spray, lipstick and other cosmetics. Stands of
clothes racks, shoes, and toys fed you to the
back of the store. Housewares were in the
back. You could smell the vinyl table cloth
that hung on rolls. Parakeets and gerbils,
turtles, and rabbits, competing with the vinyl
smell.

For Christmas, Easter or prom, special occasions, we went to New Bern or Jacksonville. I was amazed to find in high school that there were people who never left the county to go shopping or otherwise. Some never drove or owned a car.

Shopping got more complicated as I got older. When we went to Charlotte, near my grannies, the stores got bigger and so did the selections. Because I was a good student in school, I learned how to shop even better. My momma, grannies, and aunts would be proud, but not as proud as I was the day my granddaughter came up to me when we were visiting Asheville.

We took her for a week of sight-seeing. We rode Tweetsie, went to Cherokee, Santaland, Linville Caverns, and Mt. Mitchell. We swam every day in the hotel indoor pool. I was about tourist-ed out. She came to us as we woke up one morning.

"Grandma," she smiled and tugged off my covers, "I believe we need to go shopping today. I'm tired of all this other stuff."

Saturday on the Boat

House chores are finished and the grass is
cut. Sandwiches, pickles, potato salad, beer,
lemonade, cookies, napkins, paper plates,
plastic forks fill the wicker basket and
Styrofoam cooler. Life jackets, full gas tank,
anchor, and line, fishing poles, tackle box
and dried old bait shrimp, from the freezer,
packed on board. So is a tarpaulin for sitting
on or hanging over a limb for shade. Extra
line is coiled inside beneath the bow. A
change of clothes and jackets are stuffed
into a plastic bag. We tell a neighbor where
we'll be. Flash light, whistle, paddles, and
bell complete the list.

The boat – on the trailer, to the boat
ramp, hold the bow line. We know the drill.
Daddy tips the trailer and the boat slides off
carpeted shoulders. He never gets the trailer
wheels wet. She idles in the water, as we
empty and lock the station wagon. She's a
16-footer, without a name. Dad built her
himself. Mahogany varnished gunnels, white

painted topsides, green bottom. A Harkers Island bow to cut through the waves and steady the ride. A bench seat for Mom where she white knuckles the ride. She never learned how to swim.

Climb aboard. Where to today? Out to Shackleford Island to shell on the ocean side? Tag after the ponies? They let you get close, but just out of reach, before they amble away.

Cape Lockout to swim in the surf? Build castles in the sand? Fish in the ocean?

Factory Island to clam in the warm waters edging the Intracoastal Waterway?

The Inlet to bounce in the chop and try to catch a blue?

No, today is for exploring new territory, testing the waters for depth and navigability, finding an unused riverbank to sprawl out the family. Hike along steep banks cut by powerboats racing up Core Creek. Exposed roots and falling trees caused by the erosion. Driftwood, beer cans, a scrap of rag caught in a branch. Small fishing boats drift down by us. No one mentions snakes. We should have brought Dog.

Lunch spread and duly devoured. Sun lotion applied, out come the sailor hats, old tennis shoes with worn smooth soles and holey canvas tops, perfect for wading along the shore. Watch out for glass, nails, and old debris. Look up ahead, it's a cave. No. Just tired dead limbs shawled with grapevines hanging down from the exposed banks overhead. Daddy pulls a grape cluster down. We pop plump soft grapes in our mouths and taste scuppernong. I suck on the grape center until it dissolves, roll the soft flesh around in my mouth, spit out the skin and seeds. No fast food chain could offer better.

Back to the blanket to rest a bit. Put a line in the water and feed the tiny fish morsels of shrimp. Pin fish and croakers are too small to keep. Getting tired we head home. The tide changes and the Newport River kicks up. Mom puts on her life jacket and bites her bottom lip. We all settle down in the back of the boat and hold on tight. "Red on right, going south," conflicts with "red on right to port". That's the waterway chant. Give right of way to bigger faster boats. Under the bridge and up Taylor's Creek we finally dock.

At home, we unload the gear and shake out the sand. Hose down the boat and run the Evinrude in the garbage can full of water to wash out the salt. Back the trailer into the garage after the boat dries. Wash out the cooler; place it upside down in the sun. Throw out the trash; wash off the fishing poles, anchor, and line. Shower in the outside stall, washing off the sand. Tiny needles of hot water provoke the sunburn. Miniature blisters rise on shoulders and thighs. Hair squeaks clean under a vinegar rinse.

A day on the boat and we returned, salt water in our veins and sunburn on our shoulders. Memories continue building of family affairs and good times replayed in our minds, years from now.

Saturdays were filled with boating events. Floundering, fishing, diving under waves with a swim mask to see the bottom of the Cape Lookout heel. Holding my breath as long as I can, I dive deeper, ears popping until I ascend back to the surface for air. We meet other families to share the days. Their boats are skiffs or plastic look-a-like speedboats, not as pretty as ours. My Daddy made both our boats.

I never imagined my boating in years ahead. I just hold the memories, to repeat and build on. Retirement and every day can be a Saturday on the boat. (Our boat below.)

Carolina Funeral

"Will you be going to the cemetery?" A man
wearing sunglasses and somber suit directs
traffic. "Drive over there. Someone will tell
you where to park." With parade precision,
another man aligns my car behind SUVs,
pick-up trucks, and compacts.

Bikers, Vietnam veterans, dressed in
denim and leather, part as I walk through
their pack. Harnessed to one biker's saddle,
a pair of full-sized Stars and Stripes unfurls
in the breeze. Smaller flags ripple above
silver-studded saddle bags, mounted over
chrome bumpers and metal coils. The bikers
gather outside, wearing a mix of veteran
medal-decorated vests, bandanas, pony
tails, and mirrored sunglasses hide their
eyes or rest on their foreheads. Someone
guffaws, violating the funeral reverence and
whispers.

I push into the entry, "There must be several funerals going on. I didn't expect so many people."

A funeral director gently speaks, "If you're attending Mr. Kale's service, please join the line to visit with the family." It winds up one hallway across the front entry and down a second corridor.

Waiting in line, I look into rooms. A veteran lies alone, in his flag-covered open coffin. Another room contains a quiet handful of visitors, standing around a woman in her lavender coffin.

In contrast, my cousin, Butch's friends talk fondly as they crowd the passageway, wearing tee-shirts, plaid open collared shirts, flip-flops, and jeans. One man sports a navy blazer over cargo shorts.

Another Butch story starts a chuckle. A handkerchief muffles a snort. Grown men wear smiles and tears as they wait in the shrinking line. A red-eyed woman wipes her eyes and blows her nose. We hug and whisper comforting words to the sister, niece, nephew, and their spouses. Butch lies in a silver coffin. I expect him to sit up, wipe the gray from his face, and give us a punch line.

He'd smirk and tug at his recently cropped beard, "Surprise! What we gonna do next, y'all?" or "Where's the food?" He doesn't flinch, even when someone touches his face. He continues to sleep in his satin-lined box.

Two men with huge hands hug. Unchecked tears glisten on their cheeks. A country gospel version of Amazing Grace draws us into the chapel. The bearded minister introduces Butch's race car mechanic and a trucking buddy to tell us stories. A letter describes Butch as the fun-loving prankster, son, brother, military school conscript, Vietnam veteran, race car and truck driver.

As we leave the funeral home, the bikers stand in a row snapping a salute as the coffin slides into the hearse. Motorcycle engines rev. Growls increase to roars as they wheel into formation. Tattoos flex in the sunlight. Flags whip in the wind. The bikers cross the highway leading the long procession. All other traffic stops.

Piedmont towns honor and remember their dead like nowhere else. School buses, police cars, delivery vans, soccer moms, teenagers, even a riding lawn mower cease. We roll through red stoplights, down hot asphalt roads through Gastonia, across major intersections, railroad tracks, the Catawba River, red clay ditches, and countryside, into small towns like McAdenville, Lowell, Belmont, and Mt. Holly.

Wildflowers, cudzoo-draped trees, Queen Anne's lace, daisies, and honeysuckle wave as we pass. A towering magnolia tree drops a bough of blossoms. The scents of summer sneak into the car despite the closed windows.

Two waiting soft drink trucks jog my memory. Butch introduced me to Cheerwine. He shoved the bottle in my face one hot summer day, fifty years ago. At first sip, I didn't know if it was alcoholic or a cherry fruit drink. I remember his thin build, crew cut blond hair, a grin plastered across his face, and baggy clothes.

Butch grew up and didn't stop growing as a man. A couple of years back at a family reunion, his size frightened my granddaughter. His teasing and wispy beard smile won her confidence. Before the day ended, she sat in his lap.

Old men stand at attention and salute as we roll by. Some put their hand across their heart. They never knew Butch but recognize his spirit. For 40 miles, the traffic allows us passage unhindered. Cadillacs, KIAs, VW bugs, 18-wheelers, and pickup trucks halt for our long funeral parade. Cars, crawl off Interstate 85, up the ramps to wait, children poke their faces through gates to watch, and a gardener stands beside a split rail fence waving her shears.

Our final ride with Butch glides past streets named Wilkerson, Gen. Stonewall Jackson, Coral Rutledge, Mariposa, and Moses Rhyne. The cavalcade eases by his favorite burger joint, wondering if we should pull into the drive thru one last time. We slow, turning into the sprawling cemetery. Our parade of vehicles winds among silk flowers, shade trees, and granite markers.

Butch visited a friend his last day and rode his "hog" over a hill to slam into a van. Skid marks prove he tried to stop. He joked with the patrol officer, handing over his cell phone, "Call Buster, and my sister, Mary. Tell them I'm all right. I think I messed up my ankle. Can you believe that?"

The coroner said, "He died from internal injuries."

We were the same age. Butch-pictures flash in my mind, Christmas days at Granny's eating ambrosia and pound cake, picnics in the park, and cookouts.

As family sit beneath the funeral tent, the clouds climb above Spencer's Mountain and sprinkle on uncovered heads. No one flinches in the brief drizzle. I expect to hear Butch groan, buried in the same plot as his blue-haired grandmother. She was a tight-lipped, church-going widow who wore bone corsets and sturdy shoes. Or is he laughing as he squirms, spending eternity with Granny?

If there is a front porch in heaven, Butch is sitting there, watching. I can see him, one leg crossed over the other, in a chair tilted back. His hand still clutches the shower chain he pulled a few minutes before. As we head back to our cars, trucks and bikes, Butch leans his chair forward, stands up, slaps his legs, and says, "Well, boys, that was fun. What else y'all got going on up here and what time do we eat?"

To "B" or Not to "B"

To "Boat" or not to "Boat," that is the question. I married a charming live aboard, whom I lured from his boat to live ashore a few years. We sailed, for a month or so, each year for several years, heading north or south, whichever way we fancied. We cruised to Annapolis on our first long trip north and down to Beaufort, SC on our last trip south. We found, as many who have cruised before us, that it is not the destination, but the journey we enjoyed.

We took short jogs up North Carolina's Neuse, Pamlico and Bay Rivers, or Core, Bogue, and Pamlico Sounds. We cooked on the grill mounted on the stern pulpit, and watched a pod of dolphin as we hauled in the anchor one morning. Those kinds of things remembered and best shared.

My problem was that I was a Type A person. I thrived on work. I loved my business and I did it well. I had spent many years developing my trade, teaching my coworkers, and finally gotten the work down to a manageable, profitable cycle of trade and enjoyment. I was involved in church and community activities, not to mention family, who lived nearby. How could I cut back more or better yet, back out entirely? I found it became a matter of priorities. What was more important?

There were few things, so important, that you couldn't live without them. I believed a good marriage, health, faith in God, and love of family was most important. Those things traveled nicely aboard a boat. In many cases, they become stronger. That was what I learned as we cruised each year. I could leave the nine to five work pace, walk-in closets, cathedral ceilings, calendar schedules, and junk mail catalogs. I could leave the wood stove, a closet full of power suits, fancy earrings, footwear, television every night, and holiday decorations. I could leave daily newspapers, my CD player, queen size bed, and attic storage. I could leave the stream of income I'd worked so hard to build. I found we could live on less. What would I receive in return?

I would live in an area a bit bigger than most home bathrooms. I developed ingenuity and patience. I mastered creative stowage, cooking, and chart reading. Idle chatting in the marina laundry led us to a new anchorage. I now took showers in the cockpit with solar heated water. I polished the hull and stainless steel with a green scrubby, losing all my long nails. I tackled the mildew with vengeance. I practiced a new knot or finished the end of a line gone hairy. I learned to brush my teeth and wash dishes using minimal water.

I've also learned not to reinvent the wheel, living aboard. *Ibis* showed me how to make a tight mast boot. *Evergreen* showed us how to use Pampers to catch leaks. Lynn showed me how to tighten down the mainsail on the boom so that it didn't sag around in a strong blow. I noticed a good-looking set of plastic cereal containers on Jack and Annie's' Freedom. Another couple taught us to keep a clipboard, ready to jot down to-dos and a supply list for going to town.

My life completely turned around. While I live on a boat, I learned never to anticipant anything. Life isn't as I plan it. You can't keep schedules. Weather determines daily activities. A stubborn engine part can delay you a week.

I have a wardrobe of half a dozen shirts and a few pairs of shorts. I stow jeans and sweats for the colder weather. There are life preservers and rainwear where we can reach them fast. No one goes outside the cockpit, while we are underway, without a life jacket. Three pair of shoes is a closet full. My pantry is a small closet where I keep not only food, but also, pots and pans. Evenings not outdoors enjoying the sunset or strolling around a new town are spent reading or listening to good music. We hope to cruise the Hudson, the Potomac and the Florida Keys. During the winters, we'll head south and rendezvous with other boaters in the harbors and marinas.

I count my neighbors by studying anchor lights. I buy groceries, by visually deciding what can be carried back to the boat by hand or tendered by dinghy. We'll visit home for doctors and dentist appointments. We'll keep up with family and friends by email and semi-annual trips back home. I'm really looking forward to living aboard. I can do this and I know I've decided — to boat!

We Need Bridge Openings

At a time when towns are arguing with bridge opening agencies about reducing the number of openings and, better yet, replacing all open span bridges I want it to be known, I like draw bridges. This world doesn't need another four lane super highway over the next waterway.

Look around at the roadways we drive. Young parents are rushing to work. They speed in and out of breakfast, banking, childcare, and dry cleaning drive-thrus, rushing to work or school. Parents rush headlong delivering young passengers to sports, scouts, activities, and gatherings trying to include some time together. They crunch a few moments between events in hopes of quality time.

People are driving too fast these days. What happen to courtesy? I see couples rushing to hot spots to puff cigars and schmooze at the latest tasty restaurants on the coast. I see retirees chasing golf and tennis balls, rushing to concerts, or community events in hopes of grasping those last moments in a golden relationship. What this world is missing is bridge openings.

When I was a little girl growing up on the coast, a bridge opening was a special time to stop, watch, and enjoy. A big trawler or tall mast sailboat would approach a bridge. The bridge tender would flash the lights, lower the cross arms.

I can still hear the horn, whistle, and bells. Judging by the speed of the boat and the distance left to come, my father climbed out of the station wagon. Dad would encourage us to get out of the car and walk to the railing and watch the bridge, either open the draw or spin on its turnstile. It was a mechanical wonder. *We learned patience waiting for a bridge to open and close.*

Sometimes we could catch the eye of the captain and wave. Often we would get a wave back. Whether it was a marshy smell or the fragrance of an ocean breeze, we took a deep breath, inhaling the whole experience. We'd look back at the line of cars patiently waiting – to see other families doing likewise. We'd nod in recognition and enjoy the camaraderie of the moment. It was the proper thing to do, to lift a hand, and share a smile with your neighbor even for this brief minute. *We learned to respect a quiet moment shared with strangers.*

You practice to get back to the car in time to not be too late or too early in starting the engine of your car. There was definitely an art to this procedure and my father was a true artist. If he did it right, he'd put the car in gear and move forward just as the arm rose. *We learned timing and good judgment at bridge openings.*

Now I cruise in a boat along the waterway. Concrete and steel stanchions replaced most drawbridges. They are cold, quiet, and almost tomblike as we pass between their legs. No friendly bridge tenders or car travelers wave from those lofty roadways.

There are a few bridges that still open. The good ones in North Carolina include the Trent in New Bern, Williamston, Alligator River, Ocean City, and Sunset Beach, the pontoon bridge. There are wonderful bridges at Harkers Island, Great Bridge, and Elizabeth City through the Dismal Swamp Canal.

Some bridges have ruined the stopping opportunity by having a double lane converging into one lane just at the bridge. The last minute hustler trying to edge closer and save a half minute ignores people trying to wait patiently. You are afraid

to get out of your car because of the
speeders.

At others, you can take time to enjoy
them. You can walk to the edge and inhale
the breezes with your family. You have
enough time to feel the bridge move beneath
your feet. Hold hands as you walk to the side
of the bridge. Look around at the cars
behind you. Wave to the boat below and nod
at the car behind. *Relearn the joy.*

I miss those bridge openings today.
Or maybe I miss the pause of the busy road.

What do you do while the bridge
opens? Quit fiddling with your radio or cell
phone, unbuckle your seatbelt, climb out of
your car, and wave. Don't be afraid to hold
onto a spouse or child while you are nodding
to your neighbor in the cars around you. I
believe in this high speed world, we need
fewer high rise bridges and more bridges
that open.

The Storm

We are given three days warning. Forecasts
of the two fronts predict converging storms
for the west Florida coastline. One low came
from the Mexican coast where it slammed
into the other from Texas. The national
weather service and National Oceanic and
Atmospheric Administration (NOAA)
compare two models. Both bear down on the
Florida southwest coast.

The marina is full. Customary boat
readiness for a storm is carried out. Any way
water enters and leaves a floating boat is
checked. I lift the sole flooring and check the
lift lever of the electric bilge pump. All extra
canvas is taken down. Roller furling is
lashed. Loose equipment lying on deck is
secured. I notice the power boater people
bring in their deck chairs and lower their
ensigns. We visit the library for reading

material. Fresh fruit and beverages are on board.

Local and national weather people open every news program with news of the storm brewing in the Gulf of Mexico. The swirling clouds of the two low pressures are converging on the coast. If it had been a few months earlier, it would have been called a tropical depression.

The early morning buttermilk skies foretell the approaching rains. Extra fenders are placed where the increasing wind blow exposed topsides against pilings and concrete docks. Additional spring lines and chaffing gear are dug out of the locker. Wind and rain come from the east at night filling already full ditches and streams. The boat basin already high from the wind tide swells under the downpour. All night the rain hammers the deck. Pelicans and shore birds hunker down in the wind.

NOAA displays the Doppler radar. The ugly green, yellow, and red splotched fingers begin to grip the Southwest coast of Florida. Gale winds topping 50 miles an hour are predicted in local waters. The storm begins slowly to move across Florida, dragging its rains and winds.

Our boat, Wings, is a 32-foot sloop. Fully loaded she weighs less than 12,000 pounds. She is a small boat by live aboard standards. Her stern curves inward at the waterline. Her sides shear forward in the sweeping elegant line of the old-style sailing ship. The storm turned a normally well-mannered boat into a bucking animal, rearing at the waves that butt her stern; she lifts her bow above the dock. Inside I have the impression that a bull is using our stern as a battering target. The winds howl through the rigging.

I wonder how long the fiberglass hull can turn each bash into a glancing blow. Sitting comfortably or eating is impossible. Sleeping is like attempting to nap while my kid brother tries to flip me out of the hammock. I ball up in a tight knot bracing my legs and shoulders as I'm tossed from side to side. The noise and motion of the storm makes it almost impossible to sleep. Those with weak stomachs are victims of seasickness.

The temperature falls. The television newscasters showed local residents picking up fallen branches and watching eroded shorelines. A tornado touched down, flattening a trailer park. Besides a few washed over roads and the inconvenience of the rains, few Florida residents seem to notice the storm in lingering local marinas. Hurricane-like winds and rain are crashing into beaches. Red storm warning lines are drawn on the Weather Channel's maps, as far north as the Chatham, Massachusetts shoreline. Fierce snowstorms cross the Appalachian Mountains. The Ohio Valley becomes another victim of the unusual storm.

The storm continues to rock the marina for 36 hours more, but on the third day, we wake to a dead calm. No wind or waves pound the hull. We walk ashore that morning examining washed away planks on our breakwater. Lost fenders, a life jacket, and a gas can float in the mangrove hedge. Foam coats the shoreline rocks.

My father calls and tells us we are foolish to live aboard a boat. That is his way of saying he cares. My husband and I look at each other. It is sometimes hard explaining to our family and friends why we live aboard.

The Weather Channel continues to monitor the progress of the storm. Its remnants became a northeaster smashing into the New England coastline. Weather forecasters predict another low developing.

We walk to the grocery store to prepare for another blow.

My Father's Coffee Mugs

I remember the day my husband and I
walked down the road to my parent's house
to tell them I had decided to sell my
business, retire, and live on our sailboat.
Dad just looked at me and said nothing.
Over the past few years, he had humored me
with boating stories and suggestions. He
hand built our two family boats. I was raised
during the time when not every family who
lived on the coast owned a boat.

Several years prior, he sold his boat.
His eyes and ears no longer allowed him to
read the water. It was a huge change in his
lifestyle. He enjoyed keeping posted as we
sailed up the East Coast waterways during
our vacations. He had traveled much of the
same water during his Coast Guard career
and waterman's life. The next time I spoke to
Mom, she said he had asked her how old I
was. When he found out he said simply,
"Fifty, I guess she is old enough to retire."

We tried to visit them every day up until we left. One afternoon when I entered the house, he pointed over to the kitchen counter and said "There's something for your boat."

Sitting on the counter were two white, fat coffee mugs. My father never displayed any real affection for us kids. He didn't let us hug or kiss him. He never went out of his way to get me a present, before.

He found the mugs somewhere and he decided I needed them. I took an immediate dislike to these cups. They were just ugly! I planned to take the very minimum of things on board to keep life simple. I wanted to take a pair of blue enameled cups, but these new additions had me hesitating. Over the next three months, as we made trips to the boat, we carried on clothes, gear, cookware, and necessities for living aboard. Our waterline sunk deeper.

I hesitated each time I saw those mugs by the back door. I thought they might have a mishap. Perhaps they would go over the counter edge and get broken. On a final trip out of the house, I tossed the cups into the canvas carry-on bag and kept going. On board I found them a spot behind the galley stove where I could easily reach them for that cup of coffee, tea, or soup.

The lip on the cups was wider and it caused me to drip my first gulp if I wasn't careful. I noted while washing that the inside was rough. Tiny black dots were visible in the inferior glaze. I really resented those cups by the end of summer.

We planned to leave in the fall. Dad came down to the boat occasionally to see how things were going or just to talk. His back had gotten worse over the years. He walked with a stoop. Most of the time he would sit in the car or stand bent over on the dock. Coming aboard was a major undertaking.

Mid-September, we pulled away from the dock. We saw Mom and Dad the previous day when we attended their first great-grand daughter's (our grandchild's) baptism together.

During the next few months, we traveled the Intracoastal Waterway, keeping in touch by telephone and letters as we headed to Florida.

I spilled my tea in Georgetown, SC when I tried to lift one of these cups too quickly to my mouth and cursed under my breath as I watched the stain spread on my favorite shirt. The wind blew cold every day making our journey difficult. I discovered the cups kept rice and beans warm until the helmsman could take a bite while underway.

They didn't tip easily when the boat was tossed by a larger boat's wake.

The mugs are shaped like a fat little woman with a cinched in waist. The rim is as big as the widest part of the bowl. The mugs held their warmth and contents during the roughest conditions. We decide to stay the winter in Florida while El Nino blew in from the Gulf. I used the coffee mugs often. I began to see the benefits of these amazing mugs. They held the homemade potato soup perfectly, one of our favorite meals. I melted cheese over the top while the mugs smugly glared back.   Eventually I got used to seeing the mugs every time I slid open the galley shelf. I reached without animosity for them when I prepared our one pot meals.

My father's health began to decline that winter. We began our return journey late March. Dad reached us on our cellular phone to tell us he was having surgery in early April. As we headed north, the winds were always on our nose. The weather in general was miserable. Thoroughly exhausted we secured our lines in Jekyll Island, SC, to rent a car to get home sooner.

When we got to my parents, we stayed with them for several weeks during what becomes a complicated journey toward recovery for my father.

Mom losing faith in her own abilities without Dad by her side began to sit out her days. We couldn't get her to walk much farther than the dinner table. She lost all interest in her old hobbies and television soaps.

I nursed them both during the following months. I carried them to doctors' visits, fixed their meals, wiped up their spills, and cleaned up after their embarrassing accidents. Parent–child role reversal was the routine. Finally one morning my father sadly requested that we place them in a "home." He didn't want to remain a daily burden to us.

Furniture and keepsakes from 56 years of marriage moved out. A buyer made a good offer and tentatively the house sold. Mom and Dad moved into an assisted–living facility. We had time to bring our boat home.

Between visits, we noticed Dad was not getting any better. Extended stays in hospital intermediate care rooms followed midnight emergency room visits. One night I cried myself to sleep. I admitted that I knew my Daddy was dying. My husband held me closely that night. I relived all the good Daddy times: Christmases, trips in his boat, my first bicycle ride.

Mom was not prepared for what I knew was coming. During those days, she lived in a fog. Two heart attacks and a stroke took him. On his last day, we gathered around his bed. I told him I loved him and said good bye with tears running down my cheeks.

My husband and I still travel on board six months each year. We sold the sailboat and bought a small trawler. We enjoy each other's company and support more than ever. Our affection and commitment to each other has grown stronger. Living aboard still suits us. The fall weather is teasing us, hinting with cold northerly winds. Hurricane season is still with us so we won't go south for a bit. The other night we closed up the boat to keep out the wind and rain. I pulled out the polar fleece blankets and we made homemade vegetable soup. I served it in my father's coffee mugs. It was the right thing to do.

My Dear Miss Kate, a Postcard Story

*Kate Burgin was born August 25, 1887, into a
wealthy family. They owned a number of slaves
before the War Between the States. Black family's
births, marriages and deaths are listed in the Burgin
Bible along with her own family. She attended school
and displayed an interest in music. Young ladies
attended teachers' preparation college, the N. C.
Normal Institute at Asheville.*

*They wore tight waisted, ankle length skirts,
long sleeved blouses, a hat and high button shoes.
Ties, jabots, or cravats accentuated their necklines.
Class pictures show others wore a brooch or long
chain from which dangled a small-engraved watch.
Together the girls attended picnics, classes,*

chaperoned parties, socials, and reunions or homecomings of their respective towns.

There was electricity in many of their homes. Oxcarts still carried farm goods to market on the roads to Asheville. Many people rode in buggies or surreys but some early automobiles bounced through ruts, along the road. The train carried day visitors to Charlotte, Asheville, Greensboro, and points between.

Young men wore a coat, tie, vest, and always a hat, usually a felt bowler style, but in summer, a straw boater. Kate had many girlfriends. They giggled about beaus, parties, and socials. Few girls learned to cook or run a household because they all had black servants at home. Their interests are frivolous. Kate decided to transfer to Presbyterian College in Charlotte, but she still kept in touch with her friends, especially with the young men she met.

Penny postcards were a common means of communication. They were economical, fun to select because the graphics on the front neatly tied into the message each sender conveyed.

The following is a reproduction of each of her postcards. If readable, the postmark precedes each message, Kate's address, the message, the sender and a brief description of the front of each postcard she receives from 1903-1912. This writer highlights each date, postmark and the sender's name and provides year's events.

Jan 14 1903 Kings Mountain NC

Hello, Miss Kate. Reached home ok. Wish you could have been with me last night. Went to a reception. Had me grandest time and I sported your John. Now that I am at work again guess you are still selling EM. Come down and get work with John and I. Tell Mr. Reese hello. Ask him if he has learned to play cards yet. **Rossie (RK)** Front Photo of church.

*1903 Wright Brothers first flight, 1ˢᵗ Teddy Bear
introduced to market, US side of Niagara Falls runs
out of water, Caruso makes American debut.*

Feb 1904 Asheville
With best wishes for a very happy New Year. **Bess**
Front On the French Broad River, Asheville NC
Sept 1904
My horse didn't get loose last night. I'm a little bit
surprised at you. I have it in for you too. Kate like
why you came to Gastonia and didn't even say
"Howdy." Wouldn't have thought you would have
treated any body that bad and today, you didn't look a
bit guilty when I saw you at the depot. Hope you are
enjoying life to the fullest these days Try and be good
George N
Dec 12, 1904 Conover
"Wishing you a Happy Christmas" **M Loy Bolick**

*1904 US gains control of Panama Canal Zone, 1st
tunnel beneath Hudson River completed, Cy Young
pitched first perfect game in modern baseball, ice
cream cones introduced at Louisiana Purchase Expo,
Teddy Roosevelt elected.*

Feb 14, 1905 Lincolnton
Front "My heart is nailed to thine, the truth is plane,
sweet Valentine" Front Little boy nailing a
soap box shut.
July 1905 Asheville
Am going on a picnic tomorrow, come and go along
won't you? **Bess** Front Biltmore Estates
July 29, 1905 Somerset KY
Hello Kate Don't you even think enough of a fellar to
send a card sometime? **Jack** Front
Kentucky River and High Bridge Lexington Ky
Aug 1905 Atlanta
Hello Kate Am having a fine time, will write soon.
Bess Front Henry Grady Monument Atlanta, Ga
Aug 28 1905 Paducah KY

Greetings from **Jack** Front Picture of young soldier
with girl on his knee "State Militia
Encampment Field Maneuvers - Parade Rest."
Sep 1905 Asheville
Hello Kate: How are you? Aren't you surprised?
Write soon **Reece** on top of card. Hello
Miss Kate I arrived here this AM was sorry I didn't
get to see more of you at Swannanoa.
Had a fine trip but was awfully tired and sleepy.
Yours truly **Bob Sherill** front Portland Harbor
Sept 19, 1905 NC Institute Asheville
 "as I was about to leave" for the station the train
came and you didn't even look out as you passed,
well I like that! Let me know your Asheville address
please. **Loy** Front escaping convict
Oct 10, 1905 Washington DC
Having the time of my life in Wash where I want you
to come. **Loy** Front Library of Congress
Dec 28, 1905 Conover
Hello Kate Came near getting left when I left you
today but am home. Don't forget to come to Conover.
Kate don't you tell anyone about the letter writing
business. I was only joking Best wishes **Loy** Front
Photo Two men and horse and carriage.

*Kate received many kinds of post cards. She loves
violets, riding sidesaddle, and fancy* surreys, but is
beginning to gain weight, which she hates. Some of
her postcards reflect the unsaid. She despises it when
a friend sends her a card that suggests a size change,
eating, or the difficulty of catching a beau because of
her size. She often refuses to respond to the writer
who was so inconsiderate.

*1905 Russo-Japanese War Treaty signed, Einstein
submits several important papers, and Denmark and
Sweden divide into two separate countries.*

Jan 21, 1906 Conover

Hello! Are we having fun-so am coming along the
line **JDY** Front drawing of hobo along a track
walking "Coming your way"

Jan 16, 1906 Greenville SC
Front" One in a Million" **Loy** Front a pretty girl

Feb 6, 1906 Conover
NC Institute So please let me know if you are coming
to Asheville. How did you find reunion? Everything
is dead here since you left. Am invited to a
Valentines Party in Lincolnton. Would you listen if I
should write? **Loy** Front "every knock a boost"
Sledge hammer wielding worker lifting man in big
hat up in a chair with each blow.

Feb 13, 1906
NC Institute I say I will be your valentine **U G EW**
Front two kissing skaters "Wouldn't
you think it would be nice to glide with me across the
ice The ice is smooth the weather's
fine Now won't you be my Valentine?"

Feb 14,1906 Conover
Normal College Institute Asheville Unless you come
and take me out you didn't think this would ever
happen. **Loy** Front 2 policemen carrying away a man
"I may stay in this town another month."

March 7, 1906 Charlotte
C/O NC Institute Asheville Front "Carry Arms" A
young couple in arms strolling

March 24, 1906 Conover
NC Institute Kate why don't you let me hear from
you? I'll never do it again **Loy** Front A drunk falling
into flat of mortar "I'm terribly mortified."

April 11,1906 Swannanoa
C/O Reese Well I suppose you are to your Journey's
end ere. I am sure you are crazy to hear from you
know who. How did you all enjoy your trip fine, I am
sure. Hope you will have a good time be sure and
help Min to pack for Saratoga when she starts home.
Harris. Front tug of war four Dutch boys and girls
each penned by writer to say "Kate,
Minnie, Cragford and George."

April 18, 1906 Conover

NC Institute Kate do you know us? Can't you see I am angry? You certainly did snub me Wed. It's all in for you. When are you coming back? Please stop in Newton will you? **L.B.** Front a photo of two men and young woman on steps

April 30, 1906 Elrod
Guess you think I have forgotten you but you see I haven't if I waited a long time to write. Wish I was up there with you all. I had such a lovely time while there. Sorry you could not go down the station when I left Write to me soon and give my love to your sister and be sure to keep a share for yourself. **Irene Pool** Front Pansies painting

May 1906Conover
Thoughts **Loy** Front River scene Horse Shoe Bend South Fork River

June 1,1906 Statesville
C/O NC Institute Had intended coming, I really I had, but papa will be in Greensboro Tuesday, Wednesday and Thursday am awful sorry. Would like the best in the world to be there. **RMR** Front Iredell County Macadam Roads near Statesville, NC

June 2, 1906 Lincolnton
Thank you very much for the little picture you sent. It's awfully cute & I certainly appreciate. O'Hara, he has rats in his "Garret" **Sue** Write me sometime would be delighted to hear from you with the exception of Reece Front Burros and children "All well and enjoying ourselves"

Jun 20,1906 Conover
C/O AB Fortune. Not pretty but so sweet. Front "Plump person - A lady stout sure hate
To be told that she's simply great! She should be wise and exercise Before her chins double." **Loy**

June 30, 1906 York
Hello Kate! How are you? Am having a grand time here. Come up! Still angry? **M.L.B.** Front Centre Square York, PA

July 2, 1906 Statesville
"I will meet you face to face about" July 4"\ Will get into Lincolnton. On that early train if I can. Hope to

see you. Also hope you have no dates. "C" **RMR**
Front Traveling salesman with suitcase
July 14, 1906 Asheville
"I was happy until I met you" but now every day
seems a lifetime. I gave Bess the pictures to send to
you. I heard you had some good ones on me that
Mary H had told you, please write and tell them to
Bess right away. I am just crazy to know what they
are. Wish you could have been here for the doings
this week. Had a__of a time. Remember me to RH.
Ed Front Silhouette of drinking sailor "so long
Sucker"
July 1906 Asheville
Thank Mary Hoover for me - Sucker Ed said "hello"
will write you a note this evening. Tell Reese hello
for me. **Bess** Front chapel and Normal and Collegiate
Institute, Asheville
July 20, 1906 Alexander
Why don't you write to me? Are you having a good
time? Of course you are, though do write to me. I saw
Whitmore a week or so ago. Guievene Front Below
Biltmore Bridge near Asheville
July 21, 1906 Asheville
Hello Kate Mr. Wood says tell you that his looking
glass is not breaking yet. Kate do you love taffy?
They keep me from broodin' our being. I went out to
the Pain this PM and rested a while. Bess was out
there looking as sweet as you. I may come down to
God's Country about the 18th Bess and Brumfield
have been pretty busy lately. Give Reese my
love. **Ed** Front a dog scratching "A reasonable
amount of fleas is good for a dog"
July 22, 1906 Asheville
"Let me be your meal ticket" Is this the type of a
ticket Ed B should have? Am still living
and longing to see you again. **Wood** Front Meal
ticket punched.
July 26 1906 Chester SC
Hello Little Girl!! I'm thinking about you and I think
you need a ___. Did you not get my letter? Am ever
crazy to see my S.P. Please write me at Lorryville,

SC. We are spending today here. Am more than having fun now aren't you just crazy to see me??? I have so much to tell you. I ain't ever coming home. So good bye. Lots of love **Nell** Front "With all her faults I love her still" Old couple sitting

July 30,1906Wilmington, DE

What do I care about "that diamond" or seeing all of the country, ha! Do you know me? **Loy** Front Pavilion in North Park Wilmington DE

Aug 3, 1906 Asheville

Now Ed. Stop - Quit - Don't - And lets take a boat ride. **W.R.** Front Small man courting large woman on couch. His arm around her. "I must try to get around"

August 1906 Asheville

C/o JMW Hello Kate Are you going to be in Newton for the "Old Soldiers Reunion Aug 18?" Mr Wood and myself will come down, if you are in Newton that day. I saw Bess and Mr Rogers this AM How is Reece? Ed Mr. Wood sends his regards. Let me know by return mail if you expect to take it in and we will come down **Ed B Brown** Front Biltmore Estates

August 1906 Asheville

We won't go home till morning! **Bess** Front Drunk being dragged home by angry wife.

Aug 1906 Asheville

Are you too busy entertaining Reese or Mr. Hutchy? I should have said. Why don't you answer my letters Ed doesn't know one thing did you get his card. Received letter since I wrote this. Front Lovers Bridge on the Swannanoa

Aug 3,1906 Asheville

YMCA at phone 833 please **Loy** Front "Such a business" man on phone

Aug 8, 1906 Asheville

You certainly have your nerve, next time don't send my postal to 266 - see **W** Front Kissing Couple "Let me be your honey" Kate

Aug 13, 1906 Kerrs, ARK

How are you & what are you doing? **Jack** Front The Percola on the Paseo, Kansas City, MO

August 13, 1906 Lincolnton

Hello, how are you this fine morning? I hope you are
feeling better than you did the other night. I guess it
was the thought of not keeping books any longer was
it not. M.L. was over this way last night. I wish I
could have been in Lincolnton. How is Mr. G?

Sept 12, 1906 Lincolnton
Presbyterian College Here's thinking about you and
wondering what you are doing. Some one Is coming
Sat. from afar. Guess?? Hello Kate I surely do miss
you especially today. What are you doing? Do write
to me **Nell** Front Boy getting spanked "Beats the
Dutch"

Sept 1906 Asheville
Presbyterian College/ **Bess** Front Asheville
Buncombe Court House

Sep 19, 1906 Charlotte
Hello Little Kate thought you had forgotten me.
Thanks for the invite to Lincolnton only while you
are away how about coming to PC? Give the one that
knows me my love. This is sent you with my
permission only **Loy** Front 2 young men sitting on a
porch photo

*Kate's collection of postcards includes cartoons that
expressed comic thoughts from her writer friends.
Some show the African-American art characters
which were popular at that time. Others display the
horrors of love and marriage.*

Sep 1906 Charlotte
Can't you come down Friday night to the initiation? I
would love to have you. **Nettie** Front Southern view
in Albemarle Park

Sep 26, 1906 Asheville
This is for you and me. Our house is ready. Come
soon as possible. I got your letter and I will write you
a long one next week sure. Weaverville objects to
this but it does no good. I am going to the Asheville
Business College now. I am going to write you a long

one. How are you getting along in school my dear
cousin I am awful sad you did not come to
Swannanoa again. **Reese** Front Biltmore House
Oct 1906 Asheville
Presbyterian College Hello Kate! How are you
getting along in school? I am waiting for
that fine time. I haven't seen Genevieve since she
started to school. Or Lluellyn either. HA! HA! I wish
you would come up here and go to school. After
Xmas. There are some pretty girls up here but not as
pretty as you. Write soon to me. Front Silhouette of a
pretty girl "You're the girl for me"
October 2, 1906 Lincolnton
Presbyterian Hello: how are you? Saw M and Mr. L
walking yesterday afternoon. With lots of love **HAR**
Front Photo of tree lined town two stores people
walking spring.
Oct 3 1906 Moultrieville, NC
Hello Kate Am having the time of my life write to me
soon **Blanche** Front Osceola's grave Ft. Moultry,
Charleston, SC
Oct 1906 Asheville
Presbyterian College We will detain you only for a
moment" and ask you why you don't write me a line.
How are you getting along? Am coming to see you
Xmas **Bess** Front Man in stocks
Oct 16, 1906 Asheville
Presbyterian College Will tell you something funny
when I write. Hello Kate. How are you? Did you get
my last letter? Wish you were at the NC 1. I sure do
miss you Yours **Nell** PS Write me soon. Front 2
soldiers "I don't belong to the regulars, I'm just a
volunteer."
Oct 13, 1906 Charlotte
Presbyterian You know I was only teasing you just to
see what you would do. From
Guess Who Front Woman playing a piano "Dear
Miss Steinway I love to hear you pound the keys and
play a tune or two because it sounds so awfully nice
when you get through."
Oct 17, 1906 Salisbury

Hello I am having a gay time. I am in a drug store with a young lady from Asheville As ever **R** Front Big Dam near Whitney NC

Oct 29, 1906
How are the three pictures? When shall I expect the promised one? **M Loy B** Front Concordia College Conover NC

Nov 1906 Lincolnton
Presbyterian Why don't you write to me? Hope you are having a gay time Snow is fine Am over busy **J** Front Church Street Land Sweden

Going to school, traveling to expositions, and visiting friends during the holidays, Kate's days were full. She enjoys receiving postcards and letters from friends but doesn't write back as quickly. Some postcards show an interest in her studies of music. She has a fine voice and plays the piano well.

Nov 21, 1906
"My business is picking up" & I am so busy doing nothing! Letter just received and I decided to drop you a line. How is everything? I spent the day with Bess to day I am so sleepy just came home from a party. Just think Kate I haven't heard from Lora in a month. I am heart broken. You come and tell me all the news and I'll feel better. Write soon Kate Dear. **Nell** Front Beggar picking up trash and penned on coat "Ed"

Dec 11, 1906 Lincolnton
Presbyterian College I'll look for you Thursday sure but I'd much rather see you Wednesday "**C**" Come up just as soon as you arrive and I'll be seeing you soon. "**UNO**" Front Three Dutch dressed girls with a telescope looking off a dock. "You needn't look for me" "K" "N" & "L" penned on the three characters.

Dec 16, 1906 Biltmore
Presbyterian College I hope you will have a Happy Christmas From **Nell** Front 4 Black

children in Bed "Is dat a white boogey?" Penned on
each a name - Jon, Kate, Lora, Bess

Dec 1906 Matthews
Presbyterian College Kate I am going to school Wed
morning. When are you coming? Can you find
Charles on here? Wrote to me. **Bess** Cadavers photo
6 young men at tables

Dec 22, 1906 Conover
M Loy Bolick Front Holly and Berries "Brave hope
for days to be the granting of one's best desires I ask
it all for thee."

Dec 24, 1906 Maxton
"Christmas Greetings" Sincerely **Dorvis** Front Holly
and Birds

*1906 San Francisco earthquake kills 3,000, 1ˢᵗ
Victrola manufactured, SOS becomes international
call for distress.*

1907 Charlotte
Going to an all day meeting tomorrow with dinner on
the grounds, don't you want to go?
Looking for a letter from you **Ira T** Front Little boy
playing a drum on the floor pulling a
cat's tail "MUSIC."

Jan 1907 W. VA.
I will be glad to get that picture and a large one if you
have it **Wilton** Front Gateway Garden of the Gods,
Co.

Jan 1907 Laurinburg
Presbyterian College Hello Kate how are you? Don't
you hate to go back to old PC? "You mustn't pick
plums from my plum tree, 'cos I'm" saving my plums
for sweet little Kate. Lovingly **AMR** Front NY Life
cartoon policy holder and McCall 100,000 salary
under plum tree.

Jan 1907 Charlotte
How is Miss Kate tonight? I am mighty lonesome of
the gay life in Matthews. Would tike
to be with you. How long will you be at home? Will
try and come by if you will be there If you find time

you might drop me a line How did you enjoy the ride
yesterday afternoon? **DON**

Jan 3, 1907 Conover
Presbyterian College Hello Kate Thanks for the card?
Herd you didn't keep me away for L. I spent my
vacation in the valley of Va! Had a grand time you
should have been with me. Shall I expect a letter **Loy**
Front Monument of Robert E Lee, Richmond, VA

Jan 1907 Belmont
How are you Miss Kate? Just know the diamond is
all ok whether you are or not. I wrote the Lincolnton
News for samples and prices of billheads and
letterheads. As soon as I receive them I shall make an
order and have it placed to your credit. How long
does the contest last? Hope you will succeed, drop
me a card **GWS** Front St Mary's Belmont NC

Jan 18, 1907 Norfolk
Hello Kate Am on the train today to peruse our
Exhibit. It's grand. Regards **Loy** Front Pony cart and
children. "Travel in the springtime, travel in the fall
Send you thousand kisses greeting one and all."

Jan 22, 1907
Presbyterian College Letter just as soon as I find that
room Will write later to all **Nell** Front "Mid pleasures
and palaces though we may roam Be it ever so
Humble there's no place like home"

Jan 24 1907 Chapel Hill
Presbyterian College Hello Kate! I am just dropping
you this card to remind you that I have not received
that picture yet!!!! I think it is mean of you not to
send it. How is everything at PC since Xmas? Know
you are working hard(?) these days How is Mr.
Love I wonder if he is as sentimental as his name is,
ta! Tell Miss Wilkins & Kate G hello for me. Don't
work too hard **JRN** Front Greetings from Chapel Hill
basket of violets.

Jan 30, 1907 Charlotte
"That blue feeling "comes over me every since I
think of being quarantined for ten days. I talked with
Grier yesterday and she is going to call me today
about five. I have something to look forward to. I

wish you were here but don't advise you come. Write
to me and as soon as scars are covered I can see you.
We can't go to walk except on the campus even Miss
_ in shut up. I is a mess!. Thank your lucky stars you
didn't come back here I miss you very much Front a
BLUE GUY

Feb 7, 1907 Davidson
C/O Presbyterian College Hello Kate. Haven't
received that letter yet. C! Everything here covered
with snow Ole poor fishing catching it bad **RMR**
Front Shearer Hall Davidson College

Feb 11, 1907 Conover
Hello Kate! Are you in Lincolnton or Charlotte? It's
hard for me to tell! I am thinking of coming to
Lincolnton. When will you be home? Thanks for the
pictures. Its OK Let me hear from you soon **Loy**

Feb 1907 Charlotte
Presbyterian College Dear Kate: Please let me know
the day you get back to school. I want you to do an
errand for me if nothings happened- will do the best I
can on Mattie's waist. Just rec. your card this PM.
The waist hasn't come- with love **Bess**

March 2, 1907 New York NY Station
Maude Fealy signature photo of Maude Fealy

March 2, 1907 Swannanoa
Presbyterian College Hello Kate Are you still in
school, you must come up again this summer. Went
to Asheville to day to see W He is all OK **Jessie**
Front Battery Park Hotel, Asheville

March 8 1907 Charlotte
Presbyterian College We will look for you Easter
Yours Front With Best Easter Wishes

March 11 1907
What is the matter Kate? Thanks for the picture, It's
OK. **M.L.B**. Front Spooning couple kissing on the
front a drawing, Ben Franklin "Bird in the hand is
worth two in the bush"

March 12, 1907 Salisbury NC
Presbyterian College Can't you run up here & spend
some Sat & Sun with me? Would be so glad to have
you. Will let you court all you want to **Alice**

Davidson Front Court
House, Salisbury, NC

*Kate's beaus express their exasperation through
comic post cards. At other times, with deliberation
they send very romantic post cards. She dawdles in
many of her responses.*

March 26,1907
Well are you still working hard as ever I think it's
getting time for you to get someone to work for you
JBL Jr. Front Best Wishes Easter cross and violets.
March 30, 1907 Gastonia
Marie and I are down the street having a time! Mary
is taking dinner with me today wish you were too.
Marie Front we are in no hurry photo burro cart and
two young children.
April 2, 1907 Asheville
Hello Kate: What has become of you. I never hear
from you any more. Hope all of you are well. Write
to me some time. Love to all from my "husband" and
I **Bess** Front Main Street Asheville
April 14 1907 Chapel Hill
Presbyterian Dear Kate I hope that the receiving of
this by you will not result fatally for yourself not in a
surprise affliction for me. What are you doing for a
good time these days? Guess there is the usual
attraction at the Depot. I am sure that Mr. Love still
retains the attitude and in a greater degree the
sentiment of things which are suggested by his name.
I shall never forgive you for not allowing me to
become acquainted with him. I saw in the News that
you and Miss Grier were in Lincolnton for the Easter
holidays. I am sure that you had a pleasant time. I
was in Durham with Kemp and had a royal time. Met
a number of girls and some of them were real queens.
Kate I received the pictures in due time and tis
needless to say I appreciated it. It recalled vividly the
occasion of our returning to school after the Xmas
holidays. Tis just about 5 weeks now until
examinations will call us up to give an account of

ourselves and woe unto "poor me" in that day.
Wishing you happiness and much success. I remain
yours fondly **Joe R N** Front a multi-paged pictorial of
Chapel Hill
April 15, 1907 Lincolnton
Presbyterian College I see where the PC girls were
beaten again What is the matter Give Helen B my
love **Moorman** Front Courthouse Lincolnton colored
photo
April 23, 1907Asheville
Presbyterian College Hello Miss Kate I'll write you
soon **JB** Front Lovers Bridge on the Swannanoa,
Asheville, NC
May 6, 1907 Belmont
In Belmont having such a good time but Wade has
eyes for no one else since you have been here. I'm
going to write to you soon. **Nina** Front St. Mary's
College, Belmont
May 9, 1907
C/O Mrs. Burgin "I stopped on my way down" to the
station I am sorry that I did not get to tell you good
bye- Hope you will not think hard of me for it. Will
see you some time in the near future as I am so blue I
don't know what to do I only wish that school would
start gain, don't you. **DON** Front Man falling off a
ladder onto someone else.
June 1907 Charlotte
How are you little girl? Would like so much to see
you **J.B.L. Jr**. Front Red flowers
June 1907
"When I'm gone will you love me Oh yes - go" Hello
Kate How does this sink you **Loy** Front Man
threatening to leave a woman who is sitting in a chair
June 5, 1907 Gastonia
Hello Burgin! How anxious I am to see you. When
are you coming down this way? How
are you anyway? Mary Wilson spent Sat. & Sun with
me we had lots of fun Those pictuers of you all are so
cute! She gave me one of you and her. Sister has
Miss Roserusu. I thought perhaps she'd come this
week so she said . Mary got a letter for

Kate G. Wednesday. That's all to the good. Do write
me a postcard. I see where Lincolnton is to celebrate
the 4th **MarieTorrenc**e Front photo The Falls House
Hotel, Gastonia, NC

Jun 24, 1907 Richmond
Kate will be home before the 4th and hope to come to
Lincolnton what will you be doing? **Loy** Front How
does this look for a nice cemetery? 5 miles away
National Cemetery Richmond, Va.

Jun 24, 1907 Richmond
Kate will be home before the 4th and hope to come to
Lincolnton what will you be doing? **Loy** Front How
does this look for a nice cemetery? 5 miles away
National Cemetery Richmond, Va.

Jun 29, 1907 Belmont
Hello Miss Kate How are you? Please don't think that
I don't intend to write you any more for I do. Will
write before long Be real good **Geo W Stowe** Front 3
gaff rig sailing boats

June 29, 1907 Gastonia
Dear Burgin was tickled to hear from you of course
I'm coming up the 4th just for the day-hope I'll get a
glimpse of you. Mr. Tingleais coming over tomorrow
Lots of love **Marie T**.Front Telegraph Postcard
"everything coming my way" How about you? "Wish
you were"here. Got your postal yesterday am
answering on short notice. **Marie Torrence**

July 1907
What do you know about this weather. I am through
work now and will take some time sight seeing and
stocking up my suitcase Will not see Bryant this time
Clive Front Photo "My Boose'um Friend" drinking
RYE

July 5, 1907 Asheville
Dear Kate How are you why don't you let me hear
from you. With love- **Bess** Front Swannanoa River
color

July 7, 1907 Charlotte
You had better be good while I am gone **You Know**
Who Front Uncle Eph making baskets near Charlotte

July 7, 1907 Conover

Hello Kate: Am awfully sorry I didn't get to L 4th
had to go to N. Maybe I'll come to L soon How about
it? Regards to N **Loy** Front Pres. Roosevelt, Bellows
Falls VT photoJuly 1907 **0akdaleTN** Hello Kate
Does this remind you of what you might do to **ML**? I
kind of feel like I've been getting a dose like this.
Wish I could see you people celebrate the *4th* Can't
celebrate here since the towns dry JDY Front
Drawing of a big woman roller pin hanging telling
off a little man "There's no telling"

July 8 1907
A bird told me that you had a storm at your house.
No big house for me. **M.R**. Front "Just then the light
went out"

Jul 10 1907 Statesville
Hello Kate Guess you had quite a time the 4th. Wish
I could have been there. I stayed at home & did
nothing. How's everybody in Lincolnton? How do
you like our courthouse? **RMR** Front Confederate
monument courthouse, Statesville.

July 12,1907 Gastonia
Wish you were going to be at PC next year. Never
mind you can come over and visit us all. Did you
have a time the 4th? I sure did! Write soon to Marie.
Front Young girls in long bathing suits swimming
and diving at the shore, boats. Message Hello Kate
How are you? I am so sorry I didn't get to see more of
you in Lincolnton. Guess both of us were having a
time. **Marie**

July 16, 1907Asheville
Hello Miss Kate Wish you were with us here. Having
a fine time. Have you written yet? If not please do
something **GWS** Front Kenilworth Inn Asheville

July 22 1907 Mainz Holztum
sent to a USA address no signature. Front Mainz
cathedral photo

July 24, 1907 Matthews
"Chestnuts Are ripe meet me at" Matthews station
real soon and be nutty Why don't you
write to me? Do write soon. I've got lots to tell you.
Can't imagine why you haven't

answered my letter, Burgin I'm simply dying to see
you. If you love me you would come first of Aug. Let
me hear from you soon. **MT** Front "Post telegram"
July 31 1907 Fortress Monroe Va
This is a picture of our ship. We are on the Atlantic 7
miles from land the grandest sight you ever saw All
are well I having good music and grand time Hope all
are well Front US Monitor Puritan Told you where
we had planed to go did she? **Geo W. S**. Front
Richmond Capital Square
Aug 3, 1907 Asheville
Am thinking of the Phi Phi Delta giris. With love
Wallace Front Park Square Asheville
Aug 3, 1907 Waco
How is Jean today? I am just tired to death. I am not
going to W before Mon. Have just got to rest a little.
I am expecting Miss Bessie Simmonton this evening.
She is just coming for a few hours. Please let me
know about Jean **Moormouse**. Front Amusement
Park, Oceanpark near Norfolk
Aug 1907 Lincolnton
Don't think when you see this that I am in Richmond
for I am still in Belmont Why don't you write to me
some old time. Reece and I are planning a trip soon.
Miss Matie
Aug 1907 Norfolk VA
Hope you had a nice time at the ball game, wish I
could have went along **CCH** Front Jamestown
exhibition 1907 North Carolina State Building
Aug 7, 1907 Matthews
Burgin if you don't come to see me first I am going to
be mad, please come this week. The Pats are coming
if you do. And let me know before. Drop me a card
by return mail. Joe is up. Do you want to take in a
meeting? I won't play if you don't come to see me
first. I'm not selfish either and by return mail. Is Miss
Jean much better. I aint going to marry George. I
heard from E. Pat yesterday Am going but to wait for
Frid. This is me.
Mary Torrence Front Kissing wife drawing after she
buys a big hat.

August 16, 1907 Waynesville
How is this for a nice drive? Am having a glorious
time. **PIM** Front Lover's Bridge in the Land of the
Sky, colored photo.
August 16, 1907 Waynesvilte
I'll send you some cards from Waynesville. Am
having a good time **PIM** Front Looking up the
Swannanoa Valley in the land of the sky colored
photo
Aug 1907Asheville
Dear Kate Are you going to Newton Thurs. to
reunion and ball game if so please let me
know at once if you are there I will come down to
Rutherford College Wed. I thought probably you
would be at Newton, with love **Bess** FrontLake
Fairfield and Bald Rock Mt Sapphire Co. **Pat** Front
Black men Possum hunt photo
Aug 14, 1907 Charlotte
C/o Dr. Patrick Lowell Hello Burgin you ought to be
here Hope you are enjoying yourself I am going to
leave for Charlotte Tuesday. Better meet us there
Burgin I came to Charlotte Tuesday will be here until
about Friday. Can't you come by here on your way
I'm at Lula's. I'm from Atlanta. **Mary T** Front Atlanta
at night
Aug 22, 1907 Hiddenite
Am over here resting from my labors am going to
leave Charlotte in Sept for good. Wish you were here
Are you going back to Presbyterian College **Jim Mill**
Front Scene from Fern Mountain Hiddenite
Sep 2, 1907 Swannanoa
I suppose you remember this place when you use to
take me to church. Am going to write you soon.
Irene Diairdry Front All Souls Church Biltmore NC
photo

*Up until this time Miss Kate was playing the field
and having fun with her friends, and all her beaus
including George W. Stowe, M.Loy Bolick of
Conover, Reese, Jack,Don and Joe. But things begin
to happen. She is now twenty years old. She and her*

girlfriends begin to seriously think about finding
good husbands. They want to continue leisure living,
traveling and entertaining guests.

Sep 6 1907 Oceanview, Va
Wish you were with us. Having a splendid time.
Going home tonight Love from **Nina** Front1907
Jamestown Exhibition States Exhibit Palace
Sept 1907 Biltmore
Hello dear. Why don't you write to me? Hope you are
well I feel blue today We lost touch. Write me and
tell me all about yourself. I wonder if you re still
teaching music? Saw Ed today. **Mr. Joe** Front
Cartoon of a man slipping on a banana peel "Don't
wait until the fall" to write me.
Sep 11, 1907 Winston Salem
Kate I was so sorry I didn't get to tell you goodbye.
Guess Jean has told you how it all happened. Tell
Mrs. Burgin and Miss M. I'm sorry I couldn't see
them before leaving. Have been very busy since I
came back **Stell** Front Salem Female College
1907 VA
Thursday 5 I am on the Montalk on the Expo grounds
G. Wade Stowe Front Dry dock Newport News Va
1907
"I am certainly enjoying myself Hello Kate: Came to
this forsaken hole last Wednesday and wish already I
had never seen it. The sophomores have given me an
invitation to a little function tonight which I hate to
go to but will have to "C". They don't keep D pins
here. How would a pennant do? Will write tomorrow.
Hello "mino" Burgin. **GUESS**? Front Picture of child
breaking stuff.
Sept 6, 1907 Norfolk
Was out here yesterday and had a fine time. Will
leave for Baltimore this eve. **GWS** Front The surf at
Virginia Beach
Sept Winston Salem
Why don't some of you folk write to me? I am crazy
to hear from you & know how Jean is. DO hope she
is well ere this. Please write to me real soon. I am

kept right busy these days Give my love to all the family **B** Front West End Graded School Winston Salem

Sept 1907 Mt Vernon
Front Pennsylvania Ave, Washington DC **LOY**

Sep 10, 1907 Lowell
I was mighty glad to hear from you. We be at Begonia Saturday **G.W. S** Front 2 cupids holding a sign "here's to you May your joy be as deep as the ocean and your sorrow as light as the foam."

Sept 12, 1907
Does this remind you of old times **Reese** Front Charlotte NC Industrial Center. PC for Women

Sept 13, 1907 Portsmouth
Hello Kate am having the time of my life went to Cafe Charles last night on the boat & got back after 12 o'clock will send you some more cards **Susie** Front Tropical waterfalls

Sept 14, 1907 Conover
Kate, how are you? Are you going back to PC? Jms Yount and I were about to come down but I'm coming back to L. in a few weeks. I will run down and if you are down that way I lost work and looked in vain. Why not come see Susie? Tell Winni C. to come up to see me and the girls if he stops that 'Kissing Bug" business Ha. **Loy** Front USS Missouri

Sept 18 1907 Washington DC
Will be home Thursday morning expect to be on the boat all day tomorrow Leave here eight in the morning and reach Norfolk at 8 tonight. **Susie** Front US Treasury

Sept 19, 1907 Portsmouth
Hello! Kate B Though faraway, you see I think of you. **MR** Front Custom house, Norfolk VA

Sometimes the romance and whimsy of post cards digresses to buildings and places the writers are visiting or sites they are familiar with. Other times they include photographs, which was a part of Kodak's marketing to include personal photographs on penny postcards.

Sept 20 1907 Norfolk VA
Am on my way. Wish you were here to help take it
in. **Reese S**. FrontYoung girl getting kissed in a
hammock by a tennis player.
Sept 26 1907 WACO NC
BE sure to come I'm growing crazy anxious to see
you. Lots of love to all **Irene** Front Prim ugly woman
sitting on a bench with a sign "To Let"
October 1907 Charlotte
Can never tell you how much I enjoyed the candy.
You certainly are a dear. I'm going to write you
tonight 'if I can possibly get time I never had to work
so hard before **EK** Front "Would you like to Change
from Miss to Mrs" Don't be so bashful. Johnsie told
me something last night but I could hardly believe
why don't you tell me about it?
Nov 1907 Atlanta
How is old L? **C Burgin** Front Broad Street from
Marietta, Atlanta
Dec 1907 Parkton, NC
Hello Kate we are having the grandest time in our
life, company all the night- every night a crowd.
They are lovely to us. Expect to go to Fayetteville
Wed night to a play. So write my address Parkton,
NC Care of Miss Mary Mae Williams **Susie** Front
Here's thinking about you we are having a time. You
better write to me. "Just landed here" Man pulling
himself out of the water
Dec 5, 1907
How are you Miss Kate? And what are you doing?
Everyhing is OK down here The one I wrote about
last is all right Ha Write real soon Miss Kate please
Geo W S Front
Greetings from Belmont Roses
Dec 22 Conover
Coming down soon **Loy** Front Christmas sleigh and
holly.
Dec 24, 1907 Belmont
Hope you will have a mighty time during the
holidays and that your best beau will be with you **Sue**

Front Merry Christmas Bells and holly

1907 Oklahoma becomes state, Hoover vacuum invented, Montessori opens first school, 1st Native American elected to Senate, UPS founded.

Jan 11, 1908 Danville Va
"Let old acquaintance be forgotten" Guess you have forgotten me 'ere this? I still remember the good old times at the Presbyterian College in Charlotte, do you? Let me know if you are still living. Come to Danville **Jim Mills** Front Lynchburg Va Elks Lodge
Jan 13, 1908 Belmont
Isn't this grand What are you doing these times? Wish you could write to me sometimes Could you or not?
G Front Madison Park welt dressed couple.

About this time, she meets a widower, Abel Quincey Kale, a well to do entrepreneur, who writes poorly, but is wealthy. He's invested in lumber, a hot springs holiday retreat, and Aberdeen cattle. He currently manages a large textile mill. His brother was killed in a mill disagreement over workers. He is challenged into a similar dual. His gold watch catches the opponent's bullet saving his life. The fate of his opponent is unknown. He impresses her with his high social class and property holdings. She enjoys riding his horses.

Jan 10 1908 WACO NC
Hello, Miss Kate. Maybe I haven't been thinking of digging that well since I gotton home. I would give a part of my life to be with you all tonight hope you will have a nice time. You can Play my hand I am seriously thinking **Quincey Kale** Front Caskill Mt NY
Jan 27,1908 Charlotte
Why Kate everyone knew it was a joke about me telling you were to be married. They asked me why you didn't come back and I just answered them something like this 0 she's making her trouseau of

course. Ethel and Steve had to go and tease you but
you mustn't scold me next time till you have looked
the matter squarely in the face. **Johnsie** Front three
pictures of "Homes of Stuart V. Cramer, RO
Alexander and the New Hawley Residence"

Jan 23, 1908 Conover
Hello Kate! Thanks for the card thought you had
forgotten me. Think I shall come to L soon. What's
doing? Fondly M **Loy** Front Methodist Church
Hickory NC

Jan 25, 1908 Davidson
Well how is the good old burg of Lincolnton? Wish I
could be over there for a few days. They tell me it is
no longer Lincolnton but Lincoln City **RMR** Front
Imagine my surprise to get a card from you the other
day and still more to know that you have been
thinking of me?????(What did the ?s mean, that you
were just fooling?) I take it that if you were to see my
name in some matrimonial paper. I tell you Kate,
Leap Year is no good. Hasn't brought me a bit of
trade. Only had me one proposal and I had to turn it
down. **RMR** Front "Looking up his business"
Telescope maker eyeing the sky.

Feb 6, 1908
Hello Miss Kate. How is the weather? Are you
having any fun? Tis awfully dull here I think we are
going to have something doing. Your **Rossie** Front
Street of Kings Mountain

Feb 24, 1908 Greensboro
Hello Kate! Wish I could be with you now all this
afternoon instead of being cooped up at this old
place. What are you all doing for amusement these
days. Be good. We are raising the mischief. You
ought to be with us. **Peg** Front Davidson arch
Guilford Battleground

March 10, 1908 Conover
I am coming to L Friday. What will be doing for me?
On to Newton Frid and return Sat **Loy** Front
Methodist Church Hickory

April 8, 1908 Davidson
Hello Kate. How are you feeling these days since
Alien's (Mr. Miller's wedding)? Poor girl I know it
must have broken your heart. But cheer up the worst
is yet to come. You should have been there. A very
impressive service & such lovely attendants. I was
one but now that I think of it I hate why I went home.
Kate Leap year is treating me bad. Nothing doing.
RMR Front "The Male was late" Man sneaking in
house and woman at top of stairs throwing down
pots.
April 14 1908 Lenoir Lancaster

From a widower, **Guess** Front Sweetheart could I but trust you.

May 13 1908 Kings Mountain

Hello Miss Kate sure you'll be surprised to hear from me. Come down to see Rossie. We'll try and make your visit a one and am dead crazy to meet you RSVP **John Q Plorck** Front Greetings form USA Lovely ladies in the letters.

May 24 1908 Atlanta, Ga.

Hello Kate what's doing in the machine line? Has Brat been up lately? **M.R.** Front Union Depot, Atlanta, Ga.

June 1908

"Hello Miss Kate, I just bet you a one sent peace (sic) that you haven't thought of me in a year and I just can't keep ___ off my ____. I hope this an't to fresh on a card." **AQK** Front "You will sing BEDELIA - will you?"

July 1908 Montreat

Will leave this beautiful place in a few minutes and hate to go you know. **GWS** Front Still pond Montreat, NC

July 16, 1908 Atlanta

Hello Kate how are you coming on. Say come down & will take in the points if interest. You sure could have a good time. I saw an old picture of you last week. **Moorman** Front Entrance of Grant Park Atlanta

July 29, 1908 Belmont

Kate find out from Dants how she fixes those brandy peaches and let me know me know as soon as you can You and Ethel are having a good time, I am **Mattie**. Front "Here's to the land of the long leaf pine..."

Aug 5, 1908 Belmont

How is this four leaf clover Miss Kate? Will write before long. You should have been here last week we had a fine time. **G** Front Couple on a 4 leaf clover drinking "Good luck from Belmont"

Aug 6 1908 North Emporia

Hello: I am very sorry I did not get to see you before

I left. I arrived here all OK I did scarcely any last night. With all kinds of good wishes from **Paul** Front Elegant lady in Purple

Aug 16 1908 Lincolnton
Hello: I am thinking of coming to your town real soon and hope to see you. Front "To the Loved Ones Far Away"

Aug 26, 1908 Belmont
Liked your note all ok. Will do the same by you in a day or two. Hope you are enjoying the fine weather. You will please answer card. **YKW** Front St Mary's College Belmont

1908
Hello Kate. Perhaps maybe you don' think the puzzle on the other side suits the occasion but you must remember this is leap year. How have you been anyway? Do you know I never have been so lonesome before I have since I came home from Lincolnton All my bachelor friends have been knocked in the head **RMR** Front "Beam EYE Bow This is a puzzle" chalk board drawing.

Aug 29, 1908 Statesville
How's Lincolnton? Haven't heard from those parts for some time. Don't know what to think of it. Can you explain it? **RMR** Front Cannibals dancing around pot. "I'm right in it now"

Sept 3 1908 Farm School NC
Dearest Kate I didn't treat you mean for I sure wrote you last time when I was in W. Va. Why don't you come to Swannanoa to see your cousins. I think you owe me a picture don't you or at least you promised me one. W.E.A. Sure I will save a cozy for you and you alone **Wilton** Front Five scenes of Asheville

Sept 6, 1908 Statesville
Hello Kate. How are you! When do you go back to PC? I go back tomorrow then look out for some little freshman. Seems we are going to have an epidemic of weddings this fall. Never saw the like before. All my old friends are going to take the leap. **RMR** Front Statesville Female College "how do you like the looks of our institution?"

Sept 13, 1908 Drexel
Hello Sweet cousin. Why don't you come up here this
summer? Would like to see you awful bad! I think
you owe me a letter dated last year. Remember this is
your second card. Hurry up Ha Ha. I am going to
Charleston Mon **Wilton** Front Asheville Battery Park
Hotel

Sept 19, 1908 Lincolnton
C/O Miss Kirkpatrick H'lo Kate, I am just pinning
away to see you and someone else is too—Your post
looked interesting to the other party. Ahem! Do not
meet too many boys for you might have a fuss when
your pen broke. Had a grand time in NY Front
Statue of Liberty

Sep 20, 1908 Lincolnton
C/O Miss Ethel Patrick Lowell Sunday morning.
Why don't you write Jake? Jean and Sam are coming
over today The town is full of school teachers.
School opens tomorrow. Mullins gave a party Friday
night You must go with Guess. I didn't go. Hams said
they had a good time. **Mattie** Front Drawing tall well
dressed lady and short man, "I am a bit short"

Oct 9, 1908 Statesville
Have you gotten over your "complete change" (as per
postcard) yet? Don't blame you for letting your
correspondence suffer too. But let him suffer too.
Ringling Brothers circus here next Tuesday, Come!
RMR Front Chalk board drawing young man being
kicked out of house 11:45 PM "Pa saying goodnight
to sisters beau"

Oct 13, 1908 Lincolnton
Hello: I hope you enjoyed your birthday, Sunday.
Did you not? I know you. **(?)** Front Birthday
Greetings blue violets

Oct 30,1908 Salisbury
I'm sure you will be surprised to have a card from me
but I'm still in the land of the living. How are you
anyway I'm in Salisbury will be here all winter I
suppose I'm going to want to see you first chance
Jack D Front Asheville hills

Nov 25, 1908 Belmont

Miss Kate what on earth are you doing? Bet you will have a fine time Thanksgiving day. Would like to hear from you some more. Can't you write? Tell Miss Mattie Hello for me **G** Front Sacred Heart College, Belmont

Dec 13, 1908

You should have seen George smile when he read the note. Saw George a few weeks ago. Your invite is doing the work. **Mont** Front Boozer with "all sorts of things coming my way now" monsters attacking him.

Dec 16, 1908 Salisbury

P College You know I am working in Salisbury now! I am real sorry I am real sorry I didn't go down to PC Just came to Salisbury. I assure you a good time. Ida is here today You know about **M** Front US and Germany flags

Dec 16 1908 Glen Alpine NC

Hello Kate Looks now as if it will be impossible for me to reach home Thursday. You can't ever give up disappointment. Will you have anything to eat? Save til I get there. **Mont** Front "Lone Branch Girl" flapper drawing

Dec 29, 1908 Swannanoa

Dear Kate Rec'd the little package you sent and many thanks for it. It was real nice Child I am going to remember you for a while yet anyway so be patient be sure and come up next summer Will write you soon- Write soon lovingly **Jess** This is where I live Front Battery Park Hotel Asheville

1908 First year ball drops in Times Square during New Years celebration. Boy Scouts birthday, women compete in Olympics, Ford introduces Model T. Taft defeats Bryan, Butch Cassidy and Sundance Kid reported dead in South America.

Jan 23, 1909 Lincolnton
C/O Mrs John Renfrew Matthews Come home at
once **M.Burgin**. Front Cartoon singer and piano
player" Old acquaintances that should be forgotten"
Jan 24,1909 Lincolnton
Matthews Hello no doubt you are having a fine time
You ought to see H. He look as busy as I feel **R** Front
Courting couple and poem kissing.
Feb 3, 1909 Charlotte
Hello! Well I haven't heard from Thomas yet. Have
you? Edith wouldn't tell us if she did. Did you get
your package? It cost fifty cents. How did you and
"____" make it Sunday

night? Write to me soon. As ever **Lula** Front St
Mary's Catholic Church and College, Belmont
Feb13 1909
Dear Kate: Rec'd your letter and will answer soon
and many thanks for the paper. Hope you are all very
well. Wish I could see and have a "chat" this AM
With love **Bess** Front "To my True Love, Less than
half we find express, envy bid conceal the rest.
Milton"
Feb 24, 1909 Southside
Hello your note received yesterday. I will be glad to
work for you and do all I can for you. I think I can
send you a few by Sat. IWL has got the best part of
them this week but I will do my part hereafter.
Sincerely **George Rhyne** Front Young man and girl
at a well
March 1909 Washington DC
Will you remember Mar. 2, 1909 when is yours
coming off? **Adah and Laurence** Front State War &
Navy Department Washington DC
April 1909 Charlotte
My new auto what do you think of this yours **BRM**
Front Dappers in an auto
July 24, 1909 Swannanoa
Hello Kate Did you know there was a little red
headed boy living in Swannanoa? How are you
anyway sis you get my letter. I took Irene for a __
this PM had a fine time. We are having fine weather
since the day you left **JBD** Front Southern Railway
Gorge near Asheville.
Nov 7
Thank you so much for the invitation I did not get it
until I went home. Sorry I could not be there. Hope
you had a good time. I haven't heard from Poss yet I
guess he is studying mighty hard. You must come
down next year and help us to play ball **Geo Patrick**
Front Central Graded School Gastonia

*1909NAACP founded. Alice Ramsey, a 22 year old
housewife, drives across the US - first woman to do
so. US builds navel base at Pearl Harbor.*

Feb 1910 Atlanta
Do not fail to look after and fix things straight at the
C. Sunday afternoon. Wish I could be with you all.
Do not work too hard. Cold as blazes here. Front
Auto Speedway, Atlanta, Ga
March 2, 1910 Asheville
Dear Kate Bess was married today at 2PM T'was a
surprise to us alt **Nell** Front Winyah
Sanatarium, Asheville, NC

*1910 First flight of Zeppelin airships and commercial
air transportation of airplanes*

*1911 Fire at Triangle Shirtwaist Factory kills 145.
IBM incorporated in NY. Machu Picchu
rediscovered. "The Phantom of the Opera"
translated into English.*

July 10 1912 Plurntree, NC
Mrs. A Q KALE, High Shoals NC Hello girlie! How
are you these days? Would like to drop in on you
believe me— We've been having some dandy trips up
here. Don't forget me hear? Love to hear Mr. K.
mention "my Kitty" **N.M.L.** Front Roots of a large
Indian Rubber tree.

*1912 Leap Year. NM admitted as a state. 1st diesel
submarine commissioned at Groton, CT. Cracker
Jack puts prize in each box. Titanic sinks. Woodrow
Wilson wins election.*

*1913 NY City's Grand Central Station opened again.
16th Amendment ratified allowing Income Tax.
Harriet Tubman dies. 50th Anniversary of Battle of
Gettysburg draws thousands of Civil War veterans.
First crossword puzzles published in NY World
paper, Camel cigarettes introduced and modern
zipper invented. (Historical information provided by
Wikipedia.)*

Kate Burgin married Abel Quincey Kale, Jan 31, 1912. She was 25. Quincey was a widower, age 38 with an adopted daughter, age 12. Kate always called her husband, Mr. Kale. He was a wealthy textile plant manager with many investments. He was prominent in the community and associated with wealth. He frequently went with friends and workers of his mill to the bank, co-signing loans. When the depression hit the area, his name was on their notes and he lost all his fortune. His fine-bred horses, timber holdings, Aberdeen cattle, and home went to the banks. He struggled at horse-trading and remained a textile plant manager but never regained his former wealth.

Kate learned to cook for the family and did the household chores. The family lived in a home in High Shoals. Four sons and a daughter now resided in a wide porched, wooden frame home. The house caught fire and quickly burned to the ground taking with it all their furniture, linens, pictures and clothes.

Kate saved these post cards; a gold necklace Mr. Kale gave her and her parent's pictures. Everything else was lost. To marry into wealth, then lose it all must have been disappointing to her.

Later the family moved to Mt. Holly and rented a house from the Rhyne family. Kate was widowed at age 52. She was active in her church, held her head high, and managed to survive with the aid of her sons' support. One of Kate's sons, Samuel Burgin, played ball with the Rhyne boys and met Sarah Verdery Rhyne. He drove the school bus to the high school. She was at his last stop. He joined the Coast Guard, served his initial years, and returned home to Mt. Holly. They married at Sarah's home in September 1941. Sam and Sarah Kale were my parents.

Kate Burgin Kale, on her horse in High Shoals, NC., circa 1920.

The Samuel and Sarah Kale Family, 1997.